On the Outside Edge

On the Outside Edge

Being Diversions in the History of Skating

By G. Herbert Fowler

Edited by B. A. Thurber

Skating History Press

Main text originally published in 1897.

Cover image: Detail from Antoine Lafréry's colored edition (1572) of Olaus Magnus's *Carta marina et descriptio septentrionalium terrarum (Marine Map and Description of the Northern Lands)* showing skaters using bone skates.

ISBN: 978-1-948100-01-4
LCCN: 2018930019

Skating History Press
Evanston, IL
http://www.skatinghistorypress.com/

Contents

List of Figures

Introduction

Skating in the nineteenth century

The main text of this book is a brief history of skating that was first published in 1897. It chronicles the development of figure skating with emphasis on the nineteenth century, which is arguably the most interesting period in the history of figure skating because the events of that period laid the foundation for the sport. Figure skating began to emerge in the eighteenth century with Robert Jones's 1772 *Treatise on Skating*, which describes some of the movements that are still part of figure skating today. Jones's book went through several editions in the eighteenth century, but there were no substantive changes until W. E. Cormack revised it in the nineteenth century. Cormack's additions and revisions provide insight into how the sport changed during the first half of the nineteenth century.* At the beginning of the nineteenth century, figure skaters—who were usually men—prized long edges and graceful body positions. Figures in the sense of marks on the ice were in their infancy; Jones describes only one, a figure of a heart consisting of a forward outside three turn, at the end of his *Treatise*.

The first half of the nineteenth century was a relatively quiet time for skating. Cormack's substantial revision of Jones's book was published in 1855, shortly after the appearance of the first edition of *The Art of Skating* by Cyclos (George Anderson) in 1852. Cyclos foreshadowed what was to come in skating by focusing

*For details of the changes, see Thurber (2017).

on details of edges and turns and starting to classify them. This process continued with *A System of Figure Skating* by Henry Eugene Vandervell and T. Maxwell Witham, first published in 1869, and its 1881 Viennese counterpart, *Spuren auf dem Eise (Tracings on the Ice)* by Demeter Diamantidi, Carl von Korper, and Max Wirth. The title of the latter book shows how much skating had changed: the focus of the descriptions of moves shifted from expressive body positions to the marks left on the ice by skates. Body positions were still described, but they had faded into the background. Books from this era, especially *Spuren auf dem Eise*, are filled with diagrams of fantastically complex special figures made up of the basic edges and turns that are the foundation of figure skating.

On the Outside Edge mainly focuses on the development of skating in Great Britain, Fowler's homeland. He notes that many of his compatriots believed that "the art of Figure Skating was invented almost wholly in Great Britain" (25), and says nothing to contradict that statement. While Great Britain clearly had a strong influence on the development of figure skating, it was not solely responsible for the sport. In fact, during the nineteenth century, Great Britain went a different direction from the rest of Europe by developing its own special style of skating. English style skating, described by Hines (2008), is characterized by stiff, upright posture and small body movements. This style of skating has very nearly vanished, but a small remnant survives: the Royal Skating Club* still practices English style skat-

*http://www.theroyalskatingclub.co.uk/

ing in Guilford, England. Videos of the skaters can be found on YouTube. Sadly, there are no longer competitions in English style skating because so few skaters remain. It seems likely that the English style will disappear completely in the near future.

At the same time, International style skating, the direct ancestor of modern figure skating, developed on the Continent. Richardson (1956:36) attributes its origin to Jackson Haines' visit to Vienna in 1864, which Fowler discusses on pages 61–62. The difference between the two styles of skating was in the skaters' postures and movements. The International style began to take over in England in the 1890s (Hines, 2008:13).

The two styles shared many skills that are still familiar to skaters today: inside and outside edges both forward and backward, three turns, brackets, rockers, and counters. Other shared skills, like Qs, are not. Still others, like double threes, sound more familiar than they actually are (see page 100). The discovery of each of these skills was a milestone in skating history. These discoveries are chronicled in this book and tabulated beginning on page 71.

The technical and administrative sides of skating also developed rapidly during the latter half of the nineteenth century. Scientists and engineers worked on refrigeration systems that led to the first indoor ice rinks in the 1870s (Richardson, 1956:31–32). The National Ice Skating Association, which governs skating in Great Britain, was founded in 1879, and the International Skating Union (ISU), which still governs international speed and figure skating, was founded in 1892. International competitions were held before the ISU existed, but the ISU provided official administrative oversight and consistent rules for these competitions.

The ISU was also responsible for issuing the schedule of compulsory figures that skaters would be asked to perform in competitions. The figures in this schedule were standard patterns that skaters created on the ice, then went over two more times. The goal was to get the three sets of tracings as perfect—both as clean and as close—as possible. Skaters also performed free skating programs containing various tricks.

Figure skating became an Olympic sport in 1908. The events were figure skating (with separate competitions for men and ladies), pair skating, and special figures (Cook, 1909:286–287). This was the only time special figures were included in the Olympics. Because the ISU did not have any regulations governing them, the judges decided to mark the figures based on their "supposed difficulty and novelty," and "a further mark was given to the figure on the ice by each judge for the manner in which it was skated" (Cook, 1909:289). The winner was Nikolai Panin, "probably the best skater that Russia has ever produced" (Cook, 1909:290). He did not have many opponents; the only other competitors were Arthur Cumming of the United Kingdom, who placed second, and George Hall-Say, also of the United Kingdom, who placed third (Hines (2006:338), Cook (1909:287)). Irving Brokaw of the United States and Ulrich Salchow of Sweden also entered the event, but withdrew (Cook, 1909:287). In contrast, ten skaters entered the men's figure skating event, and five skaters entered the ladies' event. Panin was the only skater to compete in both compulsory and special figures (Salchow and Brokaw withdrew from the latter, and Panin withdrew from the free skating portion of the men's event) (Cook, 1909:286–287).

The small number of competitors in the special figures event suggests that as the nineteenth century closed, skaters were more interested in perfecting the compulsory figures. Skating had been systematized, and that system remains the foundation of figure skating even now that compulsory figures are no longer required in competition. The tricks and in-between skating performed by competitive skaters today owe their existence to the moves Fowler describes as milestones in the history of skating.

G. Herbert Fowler

George Herbert Fowler was born on 4 September 1861 and enrolled in Keble College, Oxford in 1880. He spent his first two years studying Greek and Latin, then changed his major to natural sciences for his final year (Bell and Stitt, 2002:249–250). After finishing his undergraduate work, Fowler continued his studies in Manchester and Leipzig, received his doctorate, and became an Assistant Professor of Zoology at University College London in 1891 (Deacon, 1984:262). He continued working as a scientist until 1919, when he became an archivist. Both phases his careers are marked by distinction.

Fowler's early adulthood was marred by a disappointing marriage. Bell and Stitt (2002:250) report that Fowler married Ursula Dewes on 20 August 1872, but this is probably a typographical error because he was only 10 years old then; the Lancashire OnLine Parish Clerk Project reports their marriage on the more reasonable date of 20 August 1885, when Fowler was 23 and Dewes was 18 (Church of St. Augustine, Pendlebury, in the County of Lancashire, 2017). Bell and Stitt (2002:250) describe the marriage as "a total failure" that "left Fowler broken-hearted and embittered" and note that Ursula Fowler left in 1892 and eventually became a medical doctor.

In graduate school and as a professor, Fowler studied marine life. He sailed on several research expeditions and designed a net for collecting organisms living in the middle layers of the ocean, which he was first able to deploy in the summer of 1896 (Deacon, 1984:262–263). The species he collected with his net allowed him to come to some conclusions about their distribution in the ocean. He found that animals tend to stay in waters of their preferred temperature; i.e., animals that live in the surface waters in the Arctic move to deeper levels, where the water is colder, at lower latitudes (Deacon, 1984:266). These and other results gave him the insight to substantially revise then-current ideas about oceanic life at medium depths (Bell and Stitt, 2002:249). He also edited *Science of the Sea* (Fowler, 1912), a book designed to teach recreational boaters to make scientific observations of the ocean (Deacon, 1984:270–271).

During World War I, Fowler volunteered in the Hydrographic Department, where he created charts of oceanographic features for submarine operators (Deacon, 1984:272). In 1919, he retired, but on his way out, he produced and promoted a plan for the continuation of his work based on the assumption that the next war would involve submarines (Deacon, 1984:273) and was appointed a Commander of the Most Excellent Order of the British Empire (CBE) (Bell and Stitt, 2002:252). Although this award shows that his work was appreciated, the plan was not followed, and Fowler's work was not continued after his retirement. Bell and Stitt (2002:249) note that "his ideas, if followed up, could probably have saved ships and lives in 1939–45."

The end of the war signaled Fowler's retirement from science. He began to focus intensely on developing the Bedfordshire County Records Office and developing new ways to organize and run archives (Deacon, 1984:284). Among the best-known results of this period of his life are *Bedfordshire in 1086: An Analysis and Synthesis of Domesday Book* (1922) and *The Care of County Muniments* (1923, with later editions following in 1928 and 1939) (Bell and Stitt, 2002:260, 254–255). He also wrote limericks that demonstrate the pronunciation of Bedfordshire place-names (Bell and Stitt, 2002:261).

Deacon (1984:271) describes Fowler's shift from scientist to archivist as "a prolonged process" that may have had its roots in his mentor's departure from University College London in 1899. Fowler applied for (and did not win) the newly vacated position. He may have focused on Bedfordshire in particular because in 1907, he moved from London to Apsley Guise. However, his book on skating history, first published in 1897, shows that his interest in history predates his move by at least a decade and his disappointment by at least two years. It goes all the way back to the time when he was studying ocean fauna with his special net.

Skating and skiing may have been the bridge between Fowler's two careers. Fowler enjoyed both winter sports for much of his life. In addition to *On the Outside Edge*, he wrote an article on the history of skiing (Fowler, 1909) and the introduction to a book on skiing (Fulton, 1911), an honor he was accorded due to his position as President of the Ski Club of Great Britain. His papers show that he was the Chairman of Committees of the Lenzerheide Ski Club in 1905, and he is known to have traveled to both Scandinavia and Switzerland in 1929 (Bell and Stitt, 2002:265). His involvement in skating is similarly extensive. Although he never won a championship, Fowler was the British representative to the ISU from 1903 to 1925 (Hines, 2011:59). According to his byline in the original edition of the present work, he was also a member of the Skating Club and of the Council of the National Skating Association.

Fowler was also very interested in medieval England and Scandinavia. When he died, he left materials about Iceland and a substantial portion of his estate to the University of Oxford. The latter was to be used to create a position for a scholar dedicated to "the 'promotion of the study of the ancient Icelandic literature and antiquities' in memory of Gudbrand Vigfusson" (Bell and Stitt, 2002:262). Fowler had admired the well-known Icelandic scholar for over 40 years; in *On the Outside Edge*, Fowler attributes "the modern revival of Scandinavian scholarship" to him (page 44). Gudbrand Vigfusson (Guðbrandur Vigfússon in Icelandic) was also responsible, with Richard Cleasby, for putting together a dictionary that has been a staple of medieval Icelandic studies for well over a century (Cleasby and Gudbrand Vigfusson, 1874). It has only recently been superseded by Degnbol et al. (2010). Fowler's expertise in this field is revealed in the discussion of references to skis in Old Norse literature in *On the Outside Edge* (pages 44–47). This section of the book may have been a first step toward his later monograph on the Domesday Book (Fowler, 1922) and other work on medieval manuscripts.

It is likely that Fowler's interests in skating, skiing,

and medieval Scandinavian studies were related. During the eighteenth and nineteenth centuries, the Vikings became extremely popular in Europe and North America, just as skating did. Medieval Scandinavian literature was romanticized and linked with skating. This like was partly due to the German poet Friedrich Gottlieb Klopstock (1724–1803). One of his poems about skating, "Die Kunst Thialfs (Thialf's Art)" attributes skating to the Norse god Thialf. Unfortunately, it is based on a mistranslation of an anecdote in the *Prose Edda*, which Fowler discusses on page 45. Closer to Fowler's time, *Frithiofs saga* (1825; see, e.g., Stromberg (1914)), a modern Swedish adaptation of an Old Norse saga, was published. The eponymous hero appears on ice wearing steel shoes, which have frequently been interpreted as ice skates (Thurber, 2011). More details of the Viking mania and its causes can be found in Wawn (2000) and Kolodny (2012).

The skating mania has not been documented as extensively, but the 1978–1979 exhibit *The American Skating Mania* at the National Museum of History and Technology made a start; an overview is provided by Lambert (1978). Fowler's book also makes a contribution to this documentation. He links skating to the popularity of medieval Scandinavia by showing where connections, both correct and mistaken, have been made. The review of *On the Outside Edge* in *The Field*, a newspaper aimed at gentlemen with country estates that included regular columns on skating during the winter months, praises it for being interesting and out of the ordinary. The reviewer's comments on it are:

The universality of figure skating as one of the arts of social life, due so very largely to the institution of real ice rinks, that render us so independent of the fickleness of winter, renders the appearance, ever and anon, of a new work dealing with the subject a matter of no surprise. A new one lies before us, and of it anything might be expected, seeing that its title is "On the Outside Edge," the author an accomplished figure skater, and the dedication to the gentleman who is well known as the much respected *doyen* of English figure skating. It is not, however, an addition to the existing stock of able treatises and instruction books on the art and its acquisition, but a highly interesting history of the development of figure skating, and, almost necessarily, the figure skate, in those countries where graceful skating is cultivated. How the iron skate came to be developed out of the original bone article of antiquity, and how it was brought to the British Isles from the Netherlands, is clearly demonstrated. Owing to the way translators have confused skates with ski, some difficulty has arisen in determining even approximately when iron-bladed skates first came into use; but they were certainly well known in the fifteenth century, though it appears to have taken a hundred years or so to introduce them

> into England, as recorded by the diarists Pepys and Evelyn. Between 1772 and 1818 a radical change came over the skate, the flat blade being curved "rocker" fashion, this telling of a demand for figure-skating purposes, and as the art became perfected, so did the niceties of blade construction, with which skaters are now familiar, develop. The credit of the first development of figure skating seems to belong to England, for as early as 1772 one Robert Jones, Lieutenant of Artillery, published a book upon its practice, whilst the Edinburgh Skating Club was certainly in existence some time before 1784, the date of the earliest minute now in existence. Mr Fowler describes the advance of the art from Jones's time, with the view of showing when and by whom new turns were invented. The difficulties of research in the case of foreign countries is, of course, great, and po[s]sibly much remains for future editions in this respect, but for as much as there is the author deserves full credit. (Anonymous, 1898:121)

On the Outside Edge was ahead of its time—and perhaps even ahead of our time. Fowler dug into the supposed references in medieval Scandinavian literature and learned that some had been discredited by scholars. He read the Dutch literature on skating and found, for example, that Buttingha-Wichers had discredited the idea that the Dutch used skates to defeat the Spaniards in 1572. Furthermore, Fowler made it clear when he was repeating something that had been said—like that Peter the Great attached blades to his boots permanently—without verification.

Skating needs more historians like Fowler. One of his stated goals is "to warn the future historian of the Art of Skating from one or two less obvious rocks" (page 26). This warning has not been taken seriously. Histories of skating still include the claim that the Dutch skated during that famous battle today, over a century after it was shown to be false. I hope that this new edition will bring Fowler's insight and warning to a new generation of skaters and historians.

This edition

In putting together this edition, I have retained Fowler's spelling and punctuation except for a few obvious errors, which I have silently corrected. I have retained Fowler's abbreviations, which are generally those still used in modern books on figure skating. They include the names of the edges (OF, IF, OB, and IB for outside forward, inside forward, outside backward, and inside backward, respectively) and numbers (3 for three turn, 8 for figure eight).

Fowler did not include the section headings in the text (except the names of countries in chapter 2), only the table of contents. I inserted them where they seemed appropriate. I moved the frontispiece to the end of Fowler's introduction, where it faces chapter 1 (page 28). References to ordinary figure numbers are to figures in this image; the numbers of the figures in the commentary are preceded by C. All footnotes in the main text are Fowler's.

The endnotes (designated by numbers rather than symbols) contain my commentary on the text. I have attempted to clarify terms that may be confusing to modern readers, provide additional information where it is of interest (including the pictures Fowler discusses but does not provide), and correct a few points on which Fowler errs. When Fowler used archaic or anglicized spellings in the text, I have generally used current ones. Unless otherwise specified, all translations are my own.

On the Outside Edge

TO

HENRY EUGENE VANDERVELL.[1]

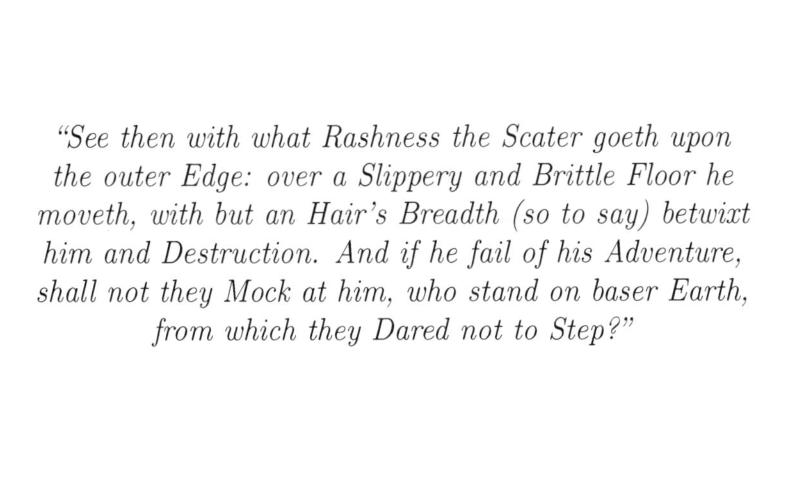

"See then with what Rashness the Scater goeth upon the outer Edge: over a Slippery and Brittle Floor he moveth, with but an Hair's Breadth (so to say) betwixt him and Destruction. And if he fail of his Adventure, shall not they Mock at him, who stand on baser Earth, from which they Dared not to Step?"

Introduction

A casual remark, which I once read in some foreign book or journal, to the effect that figure-skating had arisen in the country where the book was published (let us call it the Principality of Ruritania), jarred on the belief in which I, like other British skaters, had been nursed—the belief that, however great may be the advantages which Continental skaters enjoy by reason of regular and prolonged frost, the art of Figure Skating was invented almost wholly in Great Britain. On looking into the history of the subject I found that our old tradition was practically correct, at any rate, as far as I could check it.

I must, therefore, plead guilty to a certain insularity in maintaining that Great Britain invented figure skating for herself, even if she did not (as I believe she did) teach it largely to other nations. If this contention but stimulate skaters in other lands to study their earlier literature in order to prove me wrong, it will have done good work. It is a sporting challenge to the world, made in a spirit of friendly rivalry, as every such challenge should be made.

This booklet professes to give, not a history of figure skating (for which I have neither time nor inclination), but, at most, a comparison of the *early* progress of the art in Great Britain with that in other countries. In the later phases of development it becomes impossible to assign to each nation its due credit, owing to the increase of international communication; new ideas spread rapidly, and their history is lost at once.

Some points of antiquarian and philological interest are dealt with superficially in the following pages. Little pretence at originality is made in respect of them, yet it seemed worth while to print them for two reasons:—The first, that every skating handbook but one either omits them altogether, blunders over them, or makes sweeping and unsupported statements thereanent; the second, that they may perhaps serve to warn the future historian of the Art of Skating from one or two less obvious rocks. It is solely as a contribution to his monumental work*[2] that the present booklet is to be judged.

The one work, excepted above from the ordinary run of skating books, is the work of the late Mr. van Buttingha Wichers,† a most valuable contribution to the literary and antiquarian history of the art. As a Dutch book is a sealed book to most of us, I have not hesitated to put forward my own conclusions even when he had anticipated them.

In hunting for early books on skating, I have been necessarily limited to a great extent by the limitations of the British Museum Library, and am conscious that there must be some early books and many historical

*Geschichte des Schlittschuhlaufens: ein Beitrag zur Kenntniss der höheren Psychophysik. Von Schwingenbein Schlangenbogen; ausserordentlicher Professor der nützloser Künste in der Universität Weissnichtwo. 1900. Folio.

†J. van Buttingha Wichers, Schaatsenrijden. 'S Gravenhage, 1888. 8vo.

facts of which I am ignorant; I appeal, therefore, to my readers for corrections and additions of every kind. To the many friends who have already helped me I offer my best thanks; to the bibliography of my friend, Mr. F. W. Foster (Bibliographer, vols. 1883-4) I have been especially indebted.[3]

G. H. F.

GRAY'S INN
November, 1897.

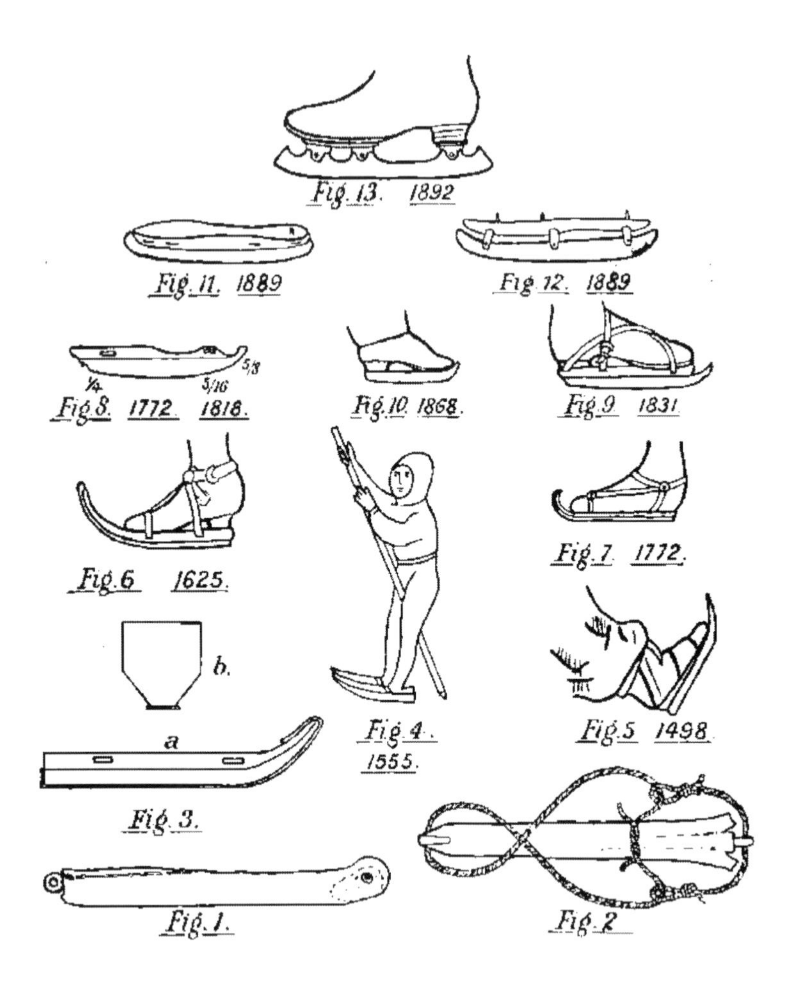

Figure I: Evolution of the English figure skate

Chapter 1. Contributions to history

The bone skate, its distribution and date, an essentially Teutonic tool

As anthropologists for the most part begin their studies with the Stone Age, so may we with the Bone Age; for the first skates of which we know, whether from actual specimens, or from references in the literature of the past, were made from bones of domestic animals. Modern ethnology, having crushed the old theory that all the white Aryan races started from the highlands of Asia, now places their cradle in central and northern Europe, along the shores of the Baltic and North Sea; it is in this area that the Bone Age of the skate was undoubtedly passed.

Bone skates have been found in Holland, North Germany, Denmark, Bavaria, Bohemia, Switzerland; and in the countries peopled by early immigrants from the Aryan cradle, England, Norway, and Sweden. In England they have only been found in the eastern counties; notably at York, Lincoln, and London. I have not been able to trace any record of their occurrence in France, Russia, or (naturally) Italy or Spain. Their distribution, therefore, so far as it goes, shows them to be Aryan, and, more particularly, Teutonic implements. Beyond these limits, the only recorded instances of similar sliding skates appear to be the use of (?) walrus teeth in Siberia,* and of Indian corn stalks by Chinese boys.†4

They have been assigned to various dates, and by some have been placed as far back as the Stone Age, on rather inadequate grounds. The latest writer‡ on the subject refuses to allow to them a greater antiquity than the Viking age; the earliest dateable find is at a town on the island of Björkö in Sweden, which is known to have existed only between the eighth and eleventh centuries of our era.

They are still in use, unchanged apparently in character, in Iceland, and in outlying parts of Bavaria, Norway, and Sweden. A modern Icelandic pair, made of the metacarpals of the cow, is in the possession of the British Museum; a second pair, made of the metacarpals of the horse, at the Pitt Rivers Collection in Oxford.[5]

The words in use for skates

Skate, Scatch, &c

The derivation of the word "skate" points also to an origin in north-western Europe. It is a member of a little family of words, most of which served at first to denote a clog or stilt—some contrivance for raising the wearer off the ground:

---

*Buttingha-Wichers, p. 73.

†*Illustrated London News*, 1861, pp. 159, 171.

‡Munro: Proc. Soc. Antiq. Scotland, xxviii. 185.

Skate* or Scatch, English.
Sketcher, Scottish.
Schaats,† modern Dutch.
Sköite,‡ modern Dano-Norwegian.
Scacia, scacci, med. Latin.
Échasse, modern French
Escache, old N.E. French.

Professor Skeat[6] kindly informs me that the old Picardy or north-eastern French word "Escache" is the oldest of these, and that it is in its turn referable to a still older Low German "Schake,"§ meaning a bone, and particularly a leg-bone or shank. It is probably a good deal more than coincidence that the oldest skates, of which we have any record, were made from the leg-bones of animals. In support of this suggestion may be urged, that the iron blade of the modern skate is still called "Schenkel" (= shank) in Holland.¶

Patin, Patten, &c

The French word for skates, "patins," does not help us much towards the history of the tool, and thus corrobo-

*The earliest citation of the word "skate" in its present sense is in Hexham's "English and Netherduytch Dictionarie," 1648 (quoted on p. 48 below).

†This word in modern sense is at least as old as 1573 (Buttingha-Wichers, p. 88).

‡Perhaps a modern application by ear of another word, connected with the Dutch "schuyt," &c. The proper Scandinavian word appears to be "skridsko" in some form or other.

§For the distribution of this word, see Grimm's Wörterbuch, *sub voce.*

¶Buttingha-Wichers, p. 72.

rates the statement with which I have met, that skating was not introduced into France till the last century (p. 62 *infra*). The word appears in a low Latin form, "patini," as early as 1295, and in its present shape as early as 1416, but them, and for long afterwards, meaning only a clog, which was often set with nails or spikes*[7] to avoid slipping on the ice. Several very early citations of the word are given in the Glossary to "Notice des Émaux du Musée du Louvre, par M. de Laborde" (Paris, 1852–3, 8vo.) *s.v.* "Patin"; but none of them seem to refer to skates, although some point to use on the ice: "Pour ferrer iij paires desdits patins pour aler sur la glace, vj s. Pour carreler iij paires des gros soulliers pour iceulx faire ferrer, chacune paire de iiij fers, à façon de fers de chevaulx et en iceulx mis iiij gros cloux à grosses pointes pour aler sur le glace." (1427.)[8]

In England also we used "patten," in the sense of a clog, for centuries:—"See, so she goeth on pattenes faire and fete."†[9] The Fenmen of to-day still use "patten" for "skate" all over the eastern counties; beyond their boundaries I have only heard of the word once, namely, in Cornwall, where my friend, Mr. Syers, gleaned the delightful phrase, "skittering on pattens." As a skating frost is a great rarity in Cornwall, the word is not likely

*Spiked clogs or cramps are still used by fishermen and sportsmen in Norway and Sweden, and are figured by Olaus Magnus. It was on cramps of this nature that the valiant Dutchmen routed the Spaniards in 1572, and not on skates (*pace* Motley), as the original description by de Mendoça shows (quoted by van Buttingha-Wichers, p. 86).

†"Court of Love," attributed to Chaucer, but written *circa* 1530.

to be indigenous, and may have been brought by the east coast fishermen, who frequent Cornish harbours in great numbers.

The earliest use of "patten" for "skate" in English, seems to be in the occasionally scandalous memoirs of the Comte d'Avaux, French Ambassador to the Netherlands. He relates* to his King that "'twas a very extraordinary thing to see the Princess of Orange, with very short petticoats, and those tucked up half way to her waist, and with iron pattins on her feet, learning to slide, sometimes on one foot, sometimes on the other," to oblige her husband and the Duke of Monmouth.[10]

It would be interesting to ascertain whether "patten" was applied to skates independently in England and France, from the not very obvious resemblance of the two implements, or whether the introduction of the word to the eastern counties was due to Huguenot immigration after the revocation of the Edict of Nantes in 1685.[11]

Skridsko, Schlittschuh, &c

The third set of words for a skate also boasts a respectable antiquity, and is traceable in Scandinavia, Germany, and England. In Middle High German we find "Schriteschuoch," and, earlier still, Scrîtscŏhe, as far back as the eleventh century, used in the sense of a seven-league boot, or shoe for flying. The proper modern High German form is "Schrittschuh," but by 1789

*Negotiations of Count d'Avaux, translated from the French. London, 1754–5. 12mo. (vol. iii., p. 132).

this had become corrupted to "Strittschuh," "Schreitschuh," "Streitschuh," and "Schlittschuh." Of these, the last has held its own against the rest, and furnishes a curious instance of the way in which a mere corruption may supplant an older form, and have a new derivation* assigned to it ("schlitten" = to slide). The word is really connected with "schreiten," and means rather a striding-shoe.[12†13] In Sweden it remains as the modern "skridsko" = skate; in England we have the word at least once as "scrickshooes."[14]

Other words

Low German and Dutch are well supplied with words for skating. We have "schovelingen" (1573), "scheuveloopen" or "scheuvelin"‡ (mod. Groningen dial.), "schöfeln" (mod. E. Friesland dial.), with many other forms, all derived from "schuiven" ("schoven") = to push or shove. "Schrenickel-schoenen"§ (1624) is probably a corruption of "schenkelschoenen" = shank-shoes, for the meaning of which see p. 31. "Reed-ride" (mod. E. Friesland) is probably the same as mod. Dutch "hard-rijden" = to ride fast.

---

*On this point Goethe and Klopstock had a friendly dispute. (Goethe: "Aus meinem Leben," bk. 15.)

†Hoole's translation of Komensky's "Orbis Sensualium Pictus," 1659.

‡Molema: Woordenboek der Groningsche Volkstaal in de 19de Eeuw. 1887.

§Buttingha-Wichers, p. 103.

Earliest mention of bone skating in England

To return to our Bone Age. The earliest literary mention of skating is an oft quoted passage from the Chronicle of FitzStephen or Stephanides (died ? 1190), the which, nevertheless, I quote once more, not only for completeness sake, but also to give the charming spelling of old Stow, the Chronicler, his translator,* generally modernised out of recognition:

> "When the great fenne or Moore† (which watereth the walles of the citie on the North side) is frozen, many young men play upon the yce, some stryding as wide as they may, doe slide swiftly . . . . some tye bones to their feete, and under their heeles, and shouing themselves by a little picked staffe, doe slide as swiftly as a birde flyeth in the aire, or an arrow out of a crossebow. Sometime two runne together with poles, and hitting one the other, eyther one or both doe fall, not without hurt; some break their armes, some their legs, but youth desirous of glorie, in this sort exerciseth it selfe against the time of warre. . . . Thus farre FitzStephen of sports."[15]

It will be noticed that this refers not to skating

*Stow: "A Survey of London," ed. 1599, p. 69.

†Moorfields, &c.

proper, but to a form of sliding only, the propulsion being obtained, not by a stroke of the skate, but a push with a picked (or pointed) staff.

Description of bone skates

By the kindness of the Curator and Assistant Curator of the Guildhall Museum, I have been able to examine a very large number of these bone skates referred to by FitzStephen; they are all made from the metacarpal bones of either horse, ass, or ox. The majority are made from the horse bones, and in the following manner:— The two condyles, or articulating surfaces, by which the bone plays on the first toe-joint, are shaved off, leaving only a natural ridge between them, to form the prow of the skate; through the latter a hole is drilled; the surface which articulates with the carpal bones is slightly trimmed square, and a hole drilled into it in the long axis of the bone, to receive a metal pin or eye; the anterior surface is then apparently ground and polished to a flat face about 9 inches long and from about $\frac{3}{8}$ to $\frac{3}{4}$ inches broad. A few of the bones were apparently used before a face had been ground to them, but in the majority of cases the flat surface is so true as to appear to be the result of deliberate grinding, and not merely of use on the ice; it shows no trace of facets.

With these bone skates are often found the lower ends of the tibiæ of horses, broken and sharpened to a point, into which probably a wooden pole was hefted to form the "little picked staffe."[16]

Two specimens in the British Museum show the

original metal loop; in one specimen this is an iron staple, set horizontally in the back end of the skate; in the other an iron loop, let into the hole, referred to above, at the back of the skate.

In the Museum at Groningen is a bone skate with three holes drilled across the bone; this was probably fastened to the foot by bands, like some modern Dutch skates.*

The woodcut of a pair of bone skates, copied into most skating manuals from Roach Smith's "Collectanea Antiqua," is utterly misleading, in apparently showing a worked ridge of bone, resembling the blade of an ordinary skate. This is due to the bad drawing of the impressions left on the metacarpal bone by the attachments of the splint-bones, or rudimentary metacarpals of the first and third toes.[17]

Good figures of these bone skates are, however, to be found in the Badminton Library volume on skating, p. 5, and in Munro's paper, already cited.†[18]

It must be remembered, however, that not all the polished bones to be seen in Museums were skates. In the Guildhall and Stockholm museums, for example, are specimens, shaped in a manner somewhat different to the shaping of the skates, which suggests that they were used as sledge runners, a board or box being laid across them. After I had arrived at the above conclusion, I was naturally pleased to find that Virchow

*Geillustreerde Catalogus van de Multiplex-Schaats. Groningen n.d. [1897].

†Proc. Roy. Soc. Antiquaries Scot., xxviii, 185.

has recorded[*] that when a boy in Pomerania, he actually possessed such a sledge; a board was nailed across the bones, on which he sat with his legs stretched out, and pushed himself along with a pair of wooden sticks shod with iron, termed "Pieken"; the whole structure forming a "Piekschlitten" (Dutch "Prickslede").[19] The Goodmans[†] saw a sledge of more or less similar character in use in the Fens as late as 1882, with a reed screen in front, to conceal a sportsman from wild duck.

In Holland, cow ribs, instead of the more usual horse bones, were in use in the last century for sliding skates.[‡]

Evolution of blade skates from skees questionable

From these bone skates, the more modern type of skate with an iron blade is in all probability derived, either directly or indirectly. A recent manual of skating[20] opens with some rather positive statements about the origin of iron skates from the Scandinavian skees[§] or snow-runners, and flatly denies that bone skates can ever have been used for skating, on the ground that it is

[*] Verhdl. Berliner Ges. Anthropol. u.s.w.. 1870. p. 19 (in Zeitschr. f. Ethnol., III.).

[†] N. and A. Goodman: "Handbook of Fen Skating." London, 1882. 8vo.

[‡] Buttingha-Wichers, p. 71.

[§] Perhaps some apology is necessary for the introduction of the word "skee" (for which, however, there is precedent). The English-coined word not only gives the correct pronunciation for a large area of Scandinavia, but allows also of a plural "skees," less pedantic than the use of the Scandinavian plurals would be.

impossible to take a stroke with them, movement on them being only obtained by pushing with a pole, in the manner so graphically described above in the quotation from FitzStephen. Unfortunately for those who dogmatise so airily, it is not impossible to take a stroke with them, for I have myself skated upon a pair of my own making—copied from the Guildhall Museum types—at the cost of many bruises, it is true; but who recks of bruises in the cause of science? Certainly a stroke cannot be taken off the side of the skate, but it can be taken off the toe, which I found quite sufficiently hard to bite on the hard ice of the National Skating Palace,[21] and which would bite even more readily on the soft outdoor English ice.[22]

It seems, therefore, far more likely that the shoeing of a bone skate with iron gave rise to the skate blade than the shoeing of skees with iron. I could not hear in Sweden of skees having been shod with iron at any time, and it is obvious that a seven-foot skee shod with iron would be a most awkward and unwieldy foot-gear. Absolutely no evidence has been produced, to my knowledge, to show when, where, or by what modifications the skee can have given rise to the skate.

In this connection, considerable weight may be attached to the statements of Archbishop Olaus Magnus, in his "Historia de Gentibus Septentrionalibus," chap. xxv. (Romae, 1555, 4to.). In the first translation into English of this stately work "by J. S." (London, 1658, 4to.), the passage runs as follows:

> "Two sorts of men are found in these places, that run Races for Wagers most swiftly. . . .

> The first is the Wild or Laplander, because upon crooked Stilts, or long Stakes fastened to the soles of his feet, he transports himself upon the Snow in Dales and Mountains, in a dangerous way, by a winding and arbitrary motion.* . . . But the other kind runs swiftly onely upon the slippery Ice, and always continues running upon the even Ice, having a plain† polished iron, or plain† Deers or Sheeps bones; namely, the shank-bones that are naturally slippery, by reason of their imbred fatness, and are a foot in length, fastened to the bottome of their feet."[23]

The passage is quite clear; there are skees for snow running only, skates of either bone or iron for ice running only; no connection between the two is suggested, even by so keen an antiquary as was the old Archbishop of Upsala.

We have, then, in history, firstly, a long period of bone skates; secondly, the introduction of a "plain" or flat "polished iron;" and lastly, the bladed skate of modern type. Is it possible to trace to-day the middle term of this series? Fortunately we can answer this question in the affirmative with some approach to probability.

*A delicious description of the wayward and wilful skees.
†Planus, *i.e.*, with a flat surface.

The snow-skate probably indicates transition from bone skate to blade-skate

In Norway and northern Sweden, when thaw followed by frost has rendered the surface of the snow impassable by skees, and also along frozen roads, communications can still be kept up by the use of a snow skate (snöskrid-sko), which seems to indicate the transition from bone or wooden runners to bladed skates.

My friend Mr. Balfour, the Keeper of the Pitt-Rivers Anthropological Collection, at Oxford, has kindly permitted me to figure (Fig. 3, *a*, *b*) one of these snow skates, of modern manufacture, which he obtained in Trondhjem some years ago. It consists of a wooden block, shaped much as the foot-gear figured in Olaus Magnus, but with the foot resting on, not slipped into, the block; under this is screwed a flat strip of polished iron $\frac{1}{2}$ inch broad and $\frac{1}{16}$ inch thick. This specimen was evidently built for a child, the length over all being $11\frac{1}{2}$, inches, the part on which the boot could rest being only $9\frac{1}{2}$ inches.*[24]

The snow-skates have been very much improved by Axel Paulsen[25] of late years, and consist in their present shape of a wooden stock, rather like a racing skate, to the running surface of which is attached a long strip of iron about 24in. long, $\frac{2}{5}$in. broad, and one-eighth inch thick. With these I am told that it is possible to make very good pace on rough ice or beaten snow tracks, the

*I am particularly indebted to Mr. Balfour for permission to figure this skate, as he himself has an article in hand on this and other early forms of skate.

edge of the iron strip being quite sufficiently sharp to allow of a firm stroke. A pole is used with them, as with skees, for rudder and brake, not for pushing.

These snow-skates seem to be nothing more or less than the Archbishop's "plain polished iron," and with them we can reconstruct the evolution of the skate with a reasonable probability. The rapid wear of the bone skates doubtless suggested the use of the more durable iron surface, affixed to wood or bone; the iron would probably at first be made broad, as like the surface of the bone skate as possible, and like the snow skates which survive in Scandinavia to-day. With this iron surface came in the possibility of a powerful stroke off its edge. It is not obvious whether the conversion of the original broad surface into the present narrow blade was effected by a gradual alteration of breadth and thickness, or by setting the iron at right angles to its original position (*evolutio per saltum*[26]); probably by the former method, if one may judge by the thickness of some old skate blades. Tradition asserts, however, that a workman, who had never seen skates, but was ordered to make a pair, ignorantly set the irons at right angles to the usual plane, and thus invented the modern blades![27]

In this connection the woodcuts in Olaus Magnus ought to be of value, but it is unfortunately doubtful how much trust can be placed in his Italian artist as regards matters of detail. In his eight woodcuts, which show either skees or skates, or both, the shape of both implements is much the same, but they differ very greatly in length.[28] Further, the skee-runner with the long footgear is always drawn on land, and has no pole; the skate runner is always drawn on ice, and carries a spiked pole, the "picked staffe" of FitzStephen. Doubt has been thrown on the correctness of shape of the skees, and if they be wrongly drawn, so perhaps are the skates also; but I would urge (1) that as they are obviously not bones, the skates are intended to represent those with "a plain polished iron"; (2) that as they are invariably accompanied by a spiked pole, of which nothing is said in the text, they were drawn under the eye of some one who knew about them, and not wholly from the artist's imagination; (3) that, this being so, they give at least an approximate picture of the earliest form of iron-shod skate. Their resemblance (Fig. 4) to the modern snow-skate is very noticeable; and it is a further argument for their being in the direct line of descent from the bone skate that, even with the iron shoeing, they were not always used for striking, at any rate in Scandinavia. So far, then, as description and drawing go, the evidence is in favour of the intermediate form between bone and blade skate, having been a strip of iron fastened to a wooden clog, such as is drawn in Fig. 3, motion being got by pushing with a spiked pole. Even before this date, as we shall see (page 47 below) a true bladed skate was in use in Holland, but it had not yet reached Scandinavia, if the artist be trustworthy. In shape these skates of Olaus Magnus, and the simpler snow-skates, lead from the nearly flat bone skate to the curved toe of the earliest bladed skate, of which a picture has come down to us. (*See* Figure I.)

Early Scandinavian references; misconceptions and mistranslations

With regard to the date of the introduction of this iron surface, we can only make a very wide approximation, based on scattered references in literature. One is frequently advised to look in the Scandinavian sagas for the earliest references to skating; but we must attribute to the neglect, with which the study of the old Scandinavian tongue has met until quite recent times, the extraordinary mistranslation of these passages from Icelandic sagas and the like, which were supposed to refer to skating, which have been copied and recopied from one skating manual to the next, but which now prove to have nothing whatever to do with the art.[29] The modern revival of Scandinavian scholarship, due in England chiefly to the late Dr. Vigfusson, of Oxford, has rendered a correction of these errors possible; the increasing popular interest in the mythology and antiquities of our Scandinavian forbears, which has become apparent of late years (excited, at any rate in part, by Wagner's powerful treatment of the Völsung myth), makes it worth while to impale, once for all, these hereditary errors of more than a century. It has not seemed to me necessary to trace the original mistakes to their sources, but the mistranslations to which I refer may be found in most text-books of skating which make any pretensions to history:

MISTRANSLATION.	TRANSLATION.
"I glide along the ice on skates"	"I can glide on skees."*
"Thialfe† answered that in running upon skates he would dispute the prize with any of the countries."	"Thialfe answered that he would try to run a race with anyone that Utgard Loke might designate."‡

(Quotation from a letter of Dr. Worsaae.[30])

"Oller, or Uller, god of winter, runs on bones of animals over the ice."	"Uller is so good an archer, and so fast on his skees, that no one can contend with him." §

*"Skriða kann-ek á skiðom": Orkneyinga Saga, ch. 61, where it is said of Earl Rognvald. Copied into Harold Sigurdsson's Mansöng (Corp. Poet. Bor. ii., 229).

†Owing to this mistranslation, Thialf has become canonised in Germany as the patron saint of skaters, since Klopstock's poem, "Die Kunst Thialfs" (1797).

‡"Þialfi segir at hann mun freista ok renna skeið nokkur við einhvern þann er Útgarda Loki faer til." Younger Edda, chap. 47 (Anderson's transl., p. 120).

§Younger Edda, ch. 31 (Anderson's transl., p. 89).

The errors have obviously arisen from taking "skið" (= a skee, or snow runner) for a skate, and then confusing it with "skeið" (= a race). The word "skið" is connected with a group of words meaning to split,* and is primarily a shingle or lath, a piece of split wood; secondarily, the long lath-like snow runner, still called "ski," or "skida," and popularly used in Norway, Sweden, and Lappland.

The only direct reference to skates proper, which I have been able to find in early Scandinavian literature, gives a totally different word—"isleggir"— (mod. Norwegian, "islaeggerne") defined in the great Cleasby-Vigfusson Dictionary as "ice legs, shin bones of sheep used for skates"; it is found in the Fornmanna Sögur.† As the manuscript in which it occurs is assigned to a date about 1320–30, this may be taken to be the earliest literary mention of skates in Scandinavia; the Saga is that of King Sigurd Jorsalfara, who died in 1130.[31]

There is also a curious passage in Saxo Grammaticus,[32] which possibly the late Dr. Worsaae had in mind when writing the letter quoted above. This tells that Oller "was such a cunning wizard that he used a certain bone, which he had marked with awful spells, wherewith to cross the seas, instead of a vessel; and that by this bone he passed over the waters that barred his way as quickly as by rowing."‡ This seems almost to

*Germ. Scheiden, Lat. Scindere, Gk. *Σχίζειν*.

†Bk. vii., p. 120 of the 1825 edition.

‡Saxo Grammaticus: Hist. Dan., bk. iii., ch. 81. (Elton's transl., p. 99.)

point to bone skates, and, as Saxo lived in Denmark about the latter half of the twelfth century, gives us yet another early reference.[33]

Earliest mention of iron skates

Taking, then, the citations from King Sigurd Jorsalfara's Saga, and from Saxo, in connection with Fitz Stephen, we may fairly infer that iron runners had not made their appearance in Scandinavia before at earliest the middle of the twelfth century. On the other hand, they were in regular use by the end of the fifteenth century in Holland, for the earliest picture of bladed skates which I can find is dated 1498,*[34] and treats of a lamentable accident.[35] There is a sort of appropriateness in the fact that the first mention and picture of our slightly dangerous pastime should relate to a catastrophe. The saintly virgin Lÿdwine, or Liedwi,[36] was knocked down on rough ice by one of her girl companions, and broke a rib. Skates are mentioned by name in the original manuscript as "tscoloedsen;" and the woodcut leaves no doubt of their having been bladed, for, although Lÿdwine's skate might almost stand for a snow-skate, the manner in which a gentleman in the background of the cut is throwing out his legs, as he skates up to her assistance, seems to imply necessarily

*Brugman: Vita Lÿdwine. Schiedam, 1498, 4to. The whole passage is deliciously graphic: "ecce una puellarū rapido cursu veniēs seseq ab ipetu cursus cohibe' nō valens: in Lÿdwinā casualiter īpegit īpactāq super fragmia glaciei dira collisioē dejicit sicq dejecte costā unā intrisecus frāgi coegit," (p. 26, not numbered).

the use of an edged blade.[37] Fig. 5 is a rough copy of Lÿdwine's foot as she lay on the ice. The accident happened in 1395, a century before the publication of the Latin translation; but it does not follow of course that the bladed skate was then in use.

Introduction of blade-skating into England

The art of skating on iron blades appears to have been introduced into England from Holland. Without providing any evidence, a recent manual of skating attributes it to the Dutch prisoners employed by Cromwell for draining fen-lands,[38] but it can be dated a little more accurately than this. Hexham, in his "English and Netherduytch Dictionarie" (1648) speaks of "skates which they slide upon the Yce in Holland;" from this we may fairly infer that they did not do so then in England. Further, Pepys, on Dec. 1, 1662, went "over the Parke (where I first in my life, it being a great frost, did see people sliding with their skeates, which is a very pretty art);" and Evelyn on the same day recorded that he saw "the strange and wonderful dexterity of the sliders on the new Canal in St. James's Park, perform'd before their Majesties by divers gentlemen and others with Scheets, after the manner of the Hollanders, with what Swiftnesse they passe, how suddainly they stop in full carriere upon the ice." There can be little doubt that it was introduced, therefore, by the Royalist exiles returning from Holland at the Restoration, and, curiously enough, we learn also from Pepys, that in 1662 was the first hard winter since the Restoration; this was the first chance that they had had of displaying their skill, since their return. It is most improbable that Pepys, always gadding about and hunting for novelties, should not have seen skaters before this date, had there been any in England. Again, Swift, writing to Stella in 1711,[39] speaks of "skates, if you know what those are." Their use can hardly have been common even at that time.

I have found no confirmation of the tradition that bladed skates were introduced by Cromwell's Dutch prisoners; nor does Dugdale, in his great "History of Imbanking and Drayning of Divers Fenns and Marshes" (1662), even mention their having been employed in such work.

Cornelius Vermuyden, the great Dutch engineer, who drained the Isle of Axholme and much of the Bedford Level, appears to have employed French and Walloon workmen. The agreement with Charles I. for his first contract is dated 1626, and he was engaged on various drainage works all over the Eastern Counties for many years; but as the natives strongly objected to his methods, broke up his sluices, made holes in his embankment, mobbed his workmen, and burned their houses over their heads, it is not likely that these poor French and Walloons had much opportunity for anything so frivolous as skating, even if they had the art.

Evolution of the English figure skate

The evolution of the English figure skate can be readily traced in the frontispiece (figure I). Fig. 1 gives a rough drawing of a bone skate of the commoner type, from the Guildhall Museum. Fig. 2 is a view of a bone skate from above, and shows the method of tying-on which I used when trying these skates, a method simplified from that of Mr. Balfour's modern Icelandic pair in the Pitt Rivers Collection.[40] Fig. 3A is an outline sketch of one of the snow-skates obtained by Mr. Balfour in Trondhjem (see p. 41), the modern survivor of Olaus Magnus' iron-shod clog, and the "missing link" between bone-skate and blade-skate. Fig. 3B is the same in section, and shows the thin broad blade at the base of a stout wooden stock. Fig. 4 is simplified from Olaus Magnus, and forms the heading to his chapter xvii., book xx. Taken with the text, this seems to represent a clog shod with a "plain polished iron," on which the old Scandinavian slid by strokes of a spiked pole.*[41] These three are only theoretically in the line of descent of our skate.

Fig. 5 is taken from the oldest printed description of a bladed skate, the "Vita Lÿdwine" of 1498 already quoted (p. 47), and may be regarded as representing the parent of all modern skates, whether for speed or figure skating. By 1625 the type had not materially altered, as may be seen from Fig. 6, taken from a print after Romeyn de Hooghe.[42] This is no doubt the type

*The spike has been added from another part of the same figure.

of skate which was introduced into England forty years later. From this point the evolution of speed and figure skates proceeds along two divergent paths, of which we are here concerned with the latter only. By 1772 had begun the shortening of the toe spike and curvature of the blade's edge, which are characteristic of figure skates.[43] These are well shown in Figs. 7 and 8, which are taken from the classic work of Lieutenant Jones.* In these days the blade tapered from toe to heel; the fractions of an inch on Fig. 8 give the thickness of the blade at three points. This figure was reprinted in the 1818 edition of Jones's hand-book. In 1831 (Fig. 9) the toe spike was almost less, the heel lengthened, the blade still tapered from toe to heel. This type, which is nearly the same as that of 1772, is to be found in the "Skater's Manual." The skates drawn by "Cyclos" (George Anderson) in 1868 are represented in Fig. 10; the toe spike has been reduced to a minimum. In addition to drawing this skate, he describes also the "club skate," with rounded toe and heel, both in the 1868 and 1852 editions. With the club skate of 1869 (Fig. 11), several types of which are to be found in the first edition of Vandervell and Witham, the toe spike had altogether vanished in England; heels were made either square or round, and longer than in the older forms; the curvature of the blade was about what it is to-day, an arc of a seven-foot radius. Skates made entirely of metal, to screw permanently to the boots, are mentioned in earlier works, and are said to have been invented by

*The English authorities here quoted are cited in full in the next chapter.

Peter the Great when in Holland.[44] The first figures of them appear in the 1869 edition of the authors last cited (Fig. 12). In Fig. 13 we have what is, on the whole, the commonest type among good skaters to-day, although a good many prefer a seven-foot radius.

Chapter 2. The rise of figure skating

The time has long gone by for honouring by name the man, greatly daring, who turned the first **3**. Like other pioneers, those who chipped the first arrow head, wore the first top-hat, and promoted the first limited company, he has passed into the Shadow of the Ages. All honour to him and in the Elysian Fields, may it be that in a quiet corner on enchanted ice, he still develops his beloved art in four or more dimensions, unfettered by gravity and the Laws of Force!

If, however, we cannot do honour by name to the actual inventor, we can at least chronicle those early masters, who, themselves proficient, made further skill possible by systematising and publishing their practice. By their aid only can we trace the gradual creation of our art out of chaos. As has been said above, Great Britain seems to have been an early nursery of the Art, as of so many other sports and pastimes. Close to her in importance come Germany and France. In Scandinavia, Austria, and Hungary, thriving as it may be to-day, skating appears to be an exotic of comparatively recent growth.

Great Britain

The earliest of the old English masters seems to have been one **Robert Jones,** Lieutenant of Artillery*; so advanced, however, is his treatise, that he must have had many keen forerunners, of whose practice he made use, and to whom, indeed, he alludes, though not by name.

He describes Inside and Outside Edges by name; the Outside Forward roll; the Spiral **(OF)**; the "Inside Circle" and "Outside Circle" (= **IF** and **OF** Spread Eagle); the "Salutation," a simple combined figure[45] in circles; the Serpentine line; the Outside backward roll; and (to my amazement) the Outside Forward **3,** which he terms "the Figure of a Heart on one Leg. This is a pleasing manœuvre, and but lately known." He also describes an **OF 8,** but not under that name. Plates of a skater in gorgeous dress, and attitudes meant to be Grecian, adorn the work.

Once planted in British soil, skating evidently thrived. Not only had a treatise on the art been published in a century from its first appearance, but a flourishing skating club bore witness to its popularity. As to the actual date of the foundation of the premier club, the **Edinburgh Skating Club,** there is some doubt. The oldest minute-book in the club's possession (for a sight of which I am indebted to the courtesy of the Committee) is dated 1784. The first entry reads: "30th January, 1784. At a meeting of the skating club . . . . it was unanimously resolved to appoint Mr. John Rae, Assis-

*Robert Jones: "A Treatise on Skating." London, 1772. 8vo.

tant Secretary to Mr. William Anderson, on account of Mr. Anderson's bad state of health." It is, therefore, obvious that the club is at least older than that date; and a list of members, "made up from memory by a quorum of the Society in January, 1778," contains the names of four who passed the entrance test of the club in that year. To pass from uncontested facts to less certain ground, there was also a tradition, inserted as such in the minutes at a much later date, that an earlier and lost minute book contained an entry to the effect that the meetings of the club were suspended in 1642, "owing to the melancholy and disturbed state of the country." To me, at least, it seems more likely that the tradition referred really to 1742 (when the country was equally disturbed), since the date 1642 does not agree with what we know of the introduction of skating into England (p. 48). It is, of course, possible that it was introduced into Scotland earlier than into England, but no evidence of this has been adduced. In this connection it is just worth notice that the writers of the article "Skating," in the "Encyclopædia Perthensis" (1816), and "Encyclopædia Metropolitana" (1845), both published in Scotland, alike refer the date of the foundation of the Edinburgh Skating Club to the last half of the eighteenth century, but not to the same year in both cases.[46]

The test for admission to the club, referred to in 1784, is not given in detail, but was probably the same as that which held in the early part of this century, namely, to skate a complete circle on either foot, and jump over first one, then two, then three hats! The last would upset a good many accomplished skaters of to-day.

Whilst on the subject of clubs, we may notice that two, which still exist, were founded in London ("The Skating Club") and Glasgow in 1830, a date far older than that of any continental club.

For some time after the appearance of Lieutenant Jones' book, which was reprinted in 1818, no great discoveries appear to have been made; indeed, the literature of 1800 to 1820 seems to indicate that the art had gone backward rather than forward. It is about this period that one frequently meets the suggestion that the outside edge should be learnt by placing a bag of lead shot in the pocket of the side to which one is to lean; and one book, which devotes a chapter to the Art of Skating, gives also directions "How to make Ice Cream!"[47]

A further advance was made by **Thomas Clay,**[*] who described the Cross Rolls forwards and backwards, and the figure Forward two turns[48] under the name of "the Turban." Yet another step forward was marked by the publication of the **"Skater's Manual,"**[†] a most excellent little work for its date (1831), this adds **OF** three turns (the "Double Three"),[49] **IF 3** and **IF** three

---

*T. Clay: "Instructions on the Art of Skating." Leeds, 1828. 8vo.

†"The Skater's Manual, or the Art of Skating" . . . . with the Sets of Quadrilles as skated on the Serpentine. By a Member of the Skating Club. London, 1831. 16mo.

turns, **OB 3** and **OB** three turns, to the skater's happiness; it also gives good directions for, and a list of, thirteen combined figures.

The foregoing works may be taken to belong to the First Period of figure skating, the empirical stage of disordered nomenclature, of isolated experiment, and of lack of method; but we enter on the transition to a new and brighter phase in 1852 with the work of **"Cyclos,"*** the pseudonym of George Anderson, for many years Member of Parliament for Glasgow. He began the task of reducing the figures to a system, and published a great many, which, if skated at all beforetime, had not hitherto been accessible in print. Among these were the **OF Q,**[50] the **OF** Reverse **Q** ("Shamrock");[51] and, the foundation of the highest branch of skating to-day—the continuous serpentine line forwards ("sea serpent") and backwards ("cork leg"). Of the continuous stroke forward, he says that it, "under a different name, was a favourite in the last century, but now it is rarely practised;" I have not, however, been able to trace it at an earlier date.

In his second edition (1868), published under his own name, he adds, Reverse two **Q's** ("United **3**"), and several figures to which he attributes a Canadian Origin, namely, the two foot continuous **8**, a grape vine, **OF** loop on the cross roll, &c.

The Modern Period begins essentially with the publication of **Vandervell and Witham's** System of Fig-

*Cyclos: "The Art of Skating." Glasgow, London, and Edinburgh, 1852. 8vo.

ure Skating,*[52] a work of the highest importance, in which the art was for the first time placed firmly upon a scientific basis, both as regarded form and matter. All the **8's,** all the **3** turns, the **Q's**, and reverse **Q's,** with combinations of multiple turns, and changes of edge, occur in this first edition, as well as a large number of simple combined figures. Further, all the Counter-rocking turns,† although still in their infancy, are lucidly described under their old name of Rocking-turns by Mr. Vandervell, who began to skate them in 1860-1861.

In the second edition of this notable work (1874) are added the elements of continuous skating in the shape of continuous **8** and continuous **Q 8.** With this edition we come to quite recent times, and may seek other sources of information than manuals.

Chief among these is the **Field** newspaper.[53] The continuous **8,** though not appearing in the first edition of Vandervell and Witham, was published here Feb. 20, 1864. The introduction of loops and a grapevine[54] from Canada is chronicled here in 1867, and in 1868 a pseudonymous skater published figures of the Cupid's bow and Crosscut.[55] These last, naturally enough, raised a great outcry. It was declared to be absolutely impossible, on both practical and theoretical grounds, to skate an "inside" curve on an outside edge, and it was asserted that the figure was only two turns in an obscured form. However, the pseudonymous skater held

*London, 1869. 8vo.

†Counters were skated on rollers by Goodrich at the Crystal Palace in 1869-70, having been independently discovered by him.

to his point, stating, in the course of the discussion, that he "first skated the figure about twenty-six years ago," that is, in 1842! Mr. Witham in 1871 furnished figures of Cross-cuts with the cut straight, concave and convex. The Mohawk step was probably introduced to England on rollers by Moe and Goodrich in 1869-70. It seems to have been then transferred from rollers to ice, and christened at the London Skating Club about 1879. In 1880 Mr. Witham, who had discovered the movement some time before, when skating on rollers, published a diagram of a bracket, and with it the continuous bracket **8** (cf. p. 66).

From Witham's "Skating Gossip"* we learn that **OF** three turns was skated by members of the Skating Club as early as 1830, and from the System of Figure Skating† that **OF Q** is older than 1849.[56]

As mentioned above, Mr. Vandervell began to work at Counters (Counter Rocking Turns) as early as 1860–1, and first published them in 1869 under the name of Rocking Turns. He tried them, as may be seen from the diagrams, both straight forward, and in the form now known as Counter Beak or Counter Pig's Ear. The invention of Rockers is not to be traced in our literature, but my friend, Mr. Montagu Monier-Williams, has kindly permitted me to publish the following extract from his letter to me on the subject:

> When Pidgeon and I were at Oxford (1878–81) the only Rocking turn then skated was Mr. Vandervell's original Counter. Pidgeon

*Badminton Magazine, i. 609.
†Ed. 1, 1869, pp. 190, 191.

> and I together worked out the Rockers in the other direction, and we were, as far as I know, the first to skate them. The new turn (now called Rocker) Pidgeon christened the Three Quarter Turn.

It was afterwards christened the Reverse Rocking Turn, then the Rocking Turn, and finally the Rocker.

Germany

From an early Encyclopaedia of Exercises and Sports, by Trichter, in 1742, we may fairly infer that skating was little, if at all, practised in Germany at that date.[57]

Thanks to the energy of the editor of *Deutscher-Eis-Sport*, in reprinting in 1895–96 selections from early German works relating to skating, there is a very good record of the history of the art in Germany.

The first publication of importance is dated 1788, and is a lecture delivered to a club of friends in Dessau, by **G. U. A. Vieth,*** a lecturer on mathematics in that town. At this date skating in Germany was evidently behind that of England, but beginning to expand. The lecture is practically devoted to big curves and spirals of outside edge, interspersed with flights of rhetoric and long quotations from Klopstock. At the end Vieth refers to further "artificialities," but dismisses them somewhat contemptuously, citing only the **OF** loop **3**,[58] the earliest mention of a loop **3** in literature. The author appears, however, to have worked

*G. U. A. Vieth: Neue Litteratur und Völkerkunde (1789), pp. 100-126. (Leipzig.)

away at his subject, for in 1795 he published a treatise on Physical Exercise,* which gives, in addition to the four edges (simple and cross), the change of edge, the spread eagle, full instructions for making letters of the alphabet in large curves, and a few numerals, including the **OF 3.**

In the first two decades of this century, the art of skating in Germany, owing presumably to the Napoleonic wars, appears to have been completely arrested in its growth, for the next work of any importance, thirty years later, by **C. S. Zindel,**† contains practically nothing which was not to be found in Vieth's book. In all probability, the renewed interest in skating, which declared itself about the middle of the century, was largely due to the appearance of a German translation of the work of **Cyclos,** referred to on p. 57 (Weimar, 1854); for it was re-issued, with additions, four years later, and may, therefore, be taken to have spread widely. A further impetus was given by the visit of Jackson Haynes to Germany and Austria in 1864–5; his performances seem to have caused profound amazement. There seems to be no doubt that this celebrated professional skater, who spent some years in Europe, awakened quite a new spirit on the Continent. So far as I can learn, he did not "catch on" in England, but in Germany, Austria, Scandinavia, and Russia, he produced a great impression. His skating appears to have been more remarkable for its strength, swing, and pace,

*G. U. A. Vieth: Versuch einer Encyclopädie der Leibesübungen. Berlin, 1795. 8vo.

†C. S. Zindel: Der Eislauf. Nuremberg, 1824 (? 1825). 8vo.

than for its introduction of new movements. My friend, Mr. Sreznevsky, of St. Petersburg, informs me that Jackson Haynes did not skate rockers, counters, and brackets; but he seems to have excelled in those movements which we still class as essentially American.[59]

The visit of Jackson Haynes to Germany was followed by the appearance of two books on figure skating in 1866, the best of which, that of **J. Zähler,*** a teacher of Gymnastics in Dresden, gives **OF 3** and Once back,[60] **OF** and **IF** two turns, **OF** and **IF Q**, a crude form of grapevine (perhaps a reminiscence of Haynes), and full instructions for numerals and letters of the alphabet; the standard, however, is by no means so high as was that of Cyclos fourteen years earlier. In 1868 **Wirth**† published figures of the reverse **Q** and of loops, which he probably took from "Cyclos," the second edition of which he quotes. After this date nothing of importance appears to have been published in Germany til 1880.[61]

France

The only statement, which I have been able to find, as to the introduction of skating into France, refers it to the eighteenth century (Sordet), and adds that in 1780, under Louis XVI., skating was a fashionable recreation. The celebrated fencer, the Chevalier de Saint-George (1745–99), is said to have been a renowned skater (Covilbeaux).[62]

---

*J. Zähler: Das Schlittschuhlaufen. Leipzig, 1866. 16mo.

†Max Wirth: Gartenlaube, 1867, p. 831; 1868, pp. 806 and 823

The first French book on skating appears to be that of **Garcin*** (1813), a work often quoted by early continental writers, but of which no copy exists, to my knowledge, in England.[63] Mr. F. W. Foster has been kind enough to prepare for me an abstract of the copy at the Bibliothèque Nationale in Paris. Garcin was very far in advance of his time; indeed, it must be admitted that, while he wrote forty years after Lieut. Jones, his book, coming just at the worst period of English skating literature, was in many points in advance of anything written on this side of the Channel for some time afterwards. He devoted himself largely, as might be expected, to steps, jumps, and poses, under highly fanciful names; but, in addition to these, he describes correctly and fully the four edges and the cross rolls, the spread-eagle ("Révérence"), **OF 8** ("Pas de huit"), **OF 3** entire ("Courtisan"), **OB 8** ("Nymphe"), some two-footed **8**s and pirouettes, the **IF** Reverse **Q** ("Venus"), the serpentine line ("Couleuvre"), On to Richmond Forwards ("Pas de Chasse"),[64] and a step for which we have no name, which consists in an inside spread-eagle immediately after **OF 3**, repeated on alternate feet. Garcin knew of double and triple turns, but does not apparently describe them in detail, nor, indeed, does he distinguish sufficiently sharply between turns and pirouettes; all except the single turn appear to have been of the nature of a spin, not of the deliberate and controlled character of a turn.

From the time of Garcin onwards, skating books published in France seem to have steadily deteriorated;

*J. Garcin: Le Vrai Patineur. Paris, 1813. 12mo.

Covilbeaux (1842), Paulin-Desormeaux (1854),[65] Silva (1857), and two anonymous writers in 1862 and 1869, are practically dilutions of Garcin in increasing weakness, and add nothing of importance to what he had already described.

The Netherlands

It is almost certain, although impossible of proof, that the first use of the Outside Edge in long curves—the "Dutch Roll"—arose in the Netherlands. To this, in all probability, the long, flat blades, which came into use in the seventeenth century,[*66] confined their wearers; for although it is possible to turn a **3** on a Friesland running skate, it would be almost impossible to discover it on them.

A description of winter sports in Holland in 1788,[†67] apparently from the pen of an eyewitness, describes long curves of outside edge; and speaks further of skaters "scratching complicated names and agreeable designs on the ice with the point of the skate." No real figures are, however, mentioned.

According to Vieth, in his works already cited above (p. 60), skaters in Holland were divided into two sects at the end of the last century: "Buten-beens-looper" (*sic*), or outside-edgers, and "Schuver," or shovers; the

---

*Balduinus: De Calceo antiquo. Amsterdam; 1667. 16mo.
†Gothaischer Hofkalender. 1788.

former aiming at grace, the latter at pace. About 1800 complex figures, made entirely of curves without turns, were skated in Holland.*[68]

Figure-skating has apparently never flourished in the Netherlands; the miles of frozen canals invite rather to long-distance journeys, or to tests of speed and endurance. Even at the Amsterdamsche Ijs Club rink, I have never seen figure-skating attempted except by Englishmen; but I am informed that it is occasionally practised, in a shamefaced sort of way, in some parts of the country.

Austria

Although Vieth's lecture, cited above, appears to have been re-published in Vienna in 1790, Figure skating in Austria seems to be only of a recent growth. Mr. Schöning, the editor of "Deutscher Eis Sport,"[69] has kindly furnished me with particulars of a book by **Fergar,**†[70] dated 1827, which describes only, in addition to the ordinary and cross edges, the serpentine line, spiral, "Mond" (probably spread-eagle), and **8**. From the account of skating in Vienna given by Silva‡ in 1857, it seems to have remained in a very rudimentary condition till that date. The authors of "Spuren auf dem Eise," a very well-known work of modern date, refer the awakening in Vienna to Jackson Haynes' visit in 1864–

*Buttingha-Wichers, p. 190; quoting J. van Geuns (1812), whose book I have unfortunately not seen.

†Fergar, F. E: Das Schlittschuhfahren. Wien, 1827. 8vo.

‡A. Silva: Sur le patin. Paris, 1857. 8vo.

5.[71] With this, of course, we arrive at modern times. I have not, unfortunately, seen the work of **Swatek,** dated 1874; but his plates of figures, published* three years later, while giving many interesting and difficult movements, deal only with various edges, **3's, Q's,** and loops; no rockers, counters, or brackets are introduced. Since that date, of course, Austria has produced (besides lesser lights) two of the best books published on figure skating—"Spuren auf dem Eise" (Diamantidi and others) and "Kunstfertigkeit im Eislaufen" (Holletschek).

The Bracket turns, as mentioned above, appear to have been worked out by Mr. Witham on roller skates. They seem, however, to have been discovered independently in Austria, for, although Mr. Witham first published them in the *Field* in 1880, all the brackets, and many combinations of brackets with other movements, are given in the first edition of "Spuren auf dem Eise" (1881). The bracket is, however, wrongly explained as containing two changes of edge, one before and one after the turn, and was probably "kicked."

In the same edition appear also "Wechselwendung" and "Verkehrte Wechselwendung," which are generally, but erroneously, translated Counter and Rocker. As a claim for priority might be urged for these, as against the true Counters and Rockers, which were first discovered and skated in England, it is worth while to translate the original description of these turns from the Austrian work:—One makes a half bracket up to

*W. Swatek: Tafeln enthaltend Schlittschuhlauf-Figuren, etc. Wien, 1877. 8vo.

the turn, without allowing a change of edge to come in after it [the turn]. By this one attains the 'Wechselwendung' . . . . In order to attain a 'Verkehrter Wechselwendung' one makes a simple three up to a point just after the turn, and then carries out a change of edge" (pp. 264-5). From this description a skater will readily see that the authors are describing, not true Rockers and Counters, but the "kicked" or **Q** form of these turns, such as most professionals on our English rinks skate. I am informed that these bastard turns are still principally skated in Vienna, although the last edition of "Spuren auf dem Eise" describes true Rockers and Counters under the names of "verkehrte gleichkantige Wendung" and "gleichkantige Wendung."*

Scandinavia

By the courtesy of Graf Snoilsky, head of the Riks Bibliothek at Stockholm, I was permitted to consult the Scandinavian books on skating in the possession of the National Library. The oldest of these proved, to my surprise, to be none other than our old friend **Cyclos**† in Swedish guise. As his translator laments the lack of a skating club in Sweden at that date, the inference is that skating was still in its infancy. This is confirmed

*These cumbrous phrases have lately been altered authoritatively to "Wende" = Rocker, and "Gegenwende" = Counter-rocker or Counter.

†Cyclos, John: Konsten att åka Skridsko. Soderhamn, 1858. 12mo.

by **Ytta**,*[72] whose book furnishes, in addition to the ordinary edges and spirals, only **IF 3, OF 3,** and two turns.

In a general handbook to Norwegian sport, **Urdahl,**† who deals at length with the history of skees, fails to produce any history of skating in Norway. He dates its modern development from the foundation of the Christiania Club in 1863, and from the visit of Jackson Haynes to Scandinavia in 1865–6.

The earliest, almost the only book in the Danish language on our subject is by **C. Höegh-Guldberg**‡[73] in 1867. This contains only **IF 3** and **OF 3** in addition to the usual edges and spirals, and represents, therefore, only a very elementary stage in the art.

Russia

Although there already existed a skating ground at St. Petersburg in connection with the Naval College, where (as I am informed by Mr. Sreznevsky) spirals, **3's,** and two turns were skated, the first skating club in Russia was founded by Englishmen in 1864, under the title of the Neva Skating Association, and appears to have given a considerable impetus to the sport. In 1863 Jackson Haynes paid his first of three visits to St. Petersburg, where, I believe, he died in 1869.[74]

From these years, 1863 and 1864, dates the rise of

*Ytta, F.: Kroppsöffningar och Lekar. Örebro, 1868. 16mo.
†Urdahl, L.: Norsk Idraet. Christiania, 1891. 4to.
‡Sköitelöberkunst. Kjöbenhavn, 1867. 16mo.

figure-skating in Russia. The first skating manual (the name of which I dare not attempt to write) is dated 1867, and appears to have been adapted from Zähler.

Switzerland

The earliest skating book published in Switzerland which I have been able to trace is that of **Sordet*** in 1873. It professedly owes a great deal to Anderson's "Art of Skating" and to Garcin, but quotes no early work of a compatriot.

Conclusion

In considering the rise of figure-skating, as sketched briefly in the foregoing pages, one thing at least is certain—that books on skating published in Great Britain, from the times of Lieutenant Jones onwards, were always well ahead of those published elsewhere, except for the meteor-like appearance of Garcin. When, with this, we take into account the two editions of Cyclos' "Art of Skating" in German, and the one in Swedish (far ahead of any books of their date), together with the wide distribution on the continent of the first (1869) edition of Vandervell and Witham, we may, I think, fairly infer that Great Britain has been, if not the Mother, at least the Governess of Continental schools of skating. Many of the early writers acknowledge their indebtedness to these sources; others, equally

*Sordet, E.: Manuel du Patineur. Geneva, 1873. 16mo.

indebted, do not. The influence of Jackson Haynes also was evidently very great abroad, some twelve or fifteen years after the publication of Cyclos' work.

The only figures which appear to have been introduced into Britain from an outside source have come to us from America*—loops from Canada, grape-vines from Canada and the United States, Mohawks (but not under their present name) from the United States. Toesteps, spins, and pirouettes can hardly be described as skating, in the English sense of the word, nor have they ever become acclimatised among us; they also are of American origin.

Great Britain may well be proud of her pupils of other lands and other tongues, in this as in so many branches of sport; let us hope that they are not wholly ungrateful to her! Is it nothing to have opened the chests, hardened the muscles, and increased the gaiety of nations? Friends and fellow-skaters—Here's luck! A votre santé, Messieurs! Prosit! Skål!

*So far as I can learn, the first serious book of American origin which deals with our subject is Swift and Clark's "Skater's Text Book" (1868). The American style, an unique growth in this, as in many other things, had evidently been evolved from the English long before this date. It became possible only when the old flat skates, imported from Germany, had been discarded, and Americans began to manufacture their own patterns. I have not found it possible to assign to the States and to Canada their respective shares in the development of figure-skating in America.

The rise of figure skating in England

Figure	Date of Publication	Authority
Spread Eagle, inside and outside edges	1772	Jones.
Eight (described, but not christened	1772	Jones.
OF Three	1772	Jones.
OF Two turns	1828	Clay.
OF Three turns	1831	Skater's Manual.
IF Three	1831	Skater's Manual.
IF Three turns	1831	Skater's Manual.
OB Three turns	1831	Skater's Manual.
OF Q	1852	Cyclos (skated before 1849, Vand. With. ed. 1869).
OF Reverse Q	1852	Cyclos.

Figure	Date of Publication	Authority
Cross-cut three	1868	Pseudonymous writer in *Field* (first skated 1842).
Other Q's	1869	Vandervell & Witham.
Other Reverse Q's	1869	Vandervell & Witham.
Counters (termed Rocking Turns)	1869	Vandervell & Witham (first skated in 1860–1).
Brackets	1880	Witham in *Field* of that year.
Rockers	1883	M. S. F. & S. F. Monier-Williams (first skated in 1878–81).
Combined Figures:		
without turns	1772	Jones.
with turns	1831	Skater's Manual.
Continuous stroke:		
forwards	1852	(Known in 18th century) Cyclos.
backwards	1852	Cyclos.
Continuous 8	1864	The *Field*.
Continuous Q 8	1874	Vandervell & Witham.

Commentary

Notes

1. Henry Eugene Vandervell (1824–1908) is well-known for his contributions to English-style skating. He and a student, T. Maxwell Witham, wrote *A System of Figure Skating*, which was one of the most detailed and popular books on skating in the nineteenth century. He also chaired the Ice Figure Committee of the National Ice Skating Association, the governing body for skating in Great Britain, from its formation in 1879/80 until his death (Hines, 2011:233).

2. The reference translates to *History of Skating: A Contribution to the Understanding of Higher Psychophysics.* By Free-leg Change-of-edge, Associate Professor of Useless Arts at the University of Whoknowswhere.

3. F. W. Foster assembled an impressive bibliography of skating books (Foster, 1898).

4. *The Illustrated London News* ran an etching with the title "Amusements on the Ice" (figure C1) on its front page and the following brief description on a later page on 23 February, 1861:

> Chinese boys on the ice.
>
> This phase of life in China forms the subject of an Engraving on our first page. "The Peiho (says our Artist in forwarding the Sketch) is frozen over, and the ponds from Pekin to Taku are solid blocks of ice, on which numerous boys disport themselves much in

> the same way that small boys do in other parts of the world. There is, however, one dodge I never saw before. A kind of skates, made of Indian-corn stalks, are placed, not fixed, under the feet, and the boys, grasping poles, shove themselves along at a glorious pace. Of course, now and then they meet with a fall, but up they get again, laughing heartily at their little accidents, and begin life afresh. Nothing can be more glorious than this steady frost, with the cloudless, clear skies, the sun shining all day, the moon all night, making the ice sparkle like diamonds, and producing a most exhilarating effect in the human frame." (Anonymous, 1861:171)

The picture and description do not quite match—the description says that the skaters did not attach their skates to their feet, but the skates of the boy who has fallen are clearly attached.

5. Research into bone skates has come a long way since Fowler published his little book. It is now generally accepted that bone skates are prehistoric in origin (though no Stone Age specimens have been found yet). The oldest bone skates found to date are from the Early Bronze Age (c. 2500 BC) and were found at Albertfalva, Hungary (Choyke and Bartosiewicz, 2005). All the earliest evidence for bone skates comes from Central

Figure C1: The etching of Chinese boys on skates published in *The Illustrated London News* in 1861 (Anonymous, 1861:159).

Europe, and they were probably invented in or near the Eurasian steppes (Küchelmann and Zidarov, 2005:430). Formenti and Minetti (2008) argue for a Finnish origin, but that hypothesis conflicts with the archaeological evidence.

Bone skates arrived in Scandinavia no later than the Migration Period, as attested by one skate found on Gotland (Stenberger, 1955:1080, 1105, 1107). At Birka, a site on the Swedish island Björkö, hundreds of skates have been found. Edberg and Karlsson (2015) describe them in detail; an English summary of the project can be found in Edberg and Karlsson (2016).

Bone skates became extremely common in areas populated by speakers of Germanic languages, especially Scandinavians, during the Middle Ages. This probably accounts for Fowler's attribution of bone skates to Teutonic peoples. Medieval bone skates have been found in all the areas mentioned by Fowler and more; since his writing, skates have been found in three of the four countries he was unable to trace: France, Russia, and Italy. They remained in use in some areas until at least 1972; Hagberg (1976:330) mentions a pair that was still in use in Iceland at that date. A database of a few thousand bone skates is available online (Küchelmann, 2011); it includes finds from France and Russia but not Italy. For Italian bone skates, see Bertolini and Hohenstein (2016).

6. Walter W. Skeat (1835–1912) is well-known in philological circles because of his contributions to the study

of the history of the English language, especially its medieval phases. His work includes his *Etymological Dictionary of the English Language* (1879–1882).

7. The myth that the Dutch used skates to defeat the Spaniards appeared as early as 1688 (Carr (1688:107, 112, 113), cited in Foster (1898:27)). It continues to be repeated to this day even though, as Fowler and Foster (1898:27) note, the original sources clearly describe crampons. Bernardino de Mendoça (1540–1605), a Spanish military officer who actually participated in various battles in the Low Countries in the 1560s and 1570s, wrote extensive commentary on what happened. He describes the Dutch using shoes "con dos ramploncillos en forma de puntas de diamante en vna planchilla de yerro" (with two sharp spikes in the form of points of a diamond on an iron plate) that allowed them to walk and fight on the ice without sliding (de Mendoza, 1592:173). They are clearly not skates.

8. This quotation is from a receipt cited in Beaulieu and Baylé (1956:91, 93). It translates roughly to "To shoe 3 pairs of said patins to go on ice, 6 s. To mend 3 pairs of large shoes for that, nail to each pair 4 irons in the shape of a horseshoe, and onto it put 4 large spikes with large points to go on the ice." An illustrated discussion (in Dutch) of the use of pattens for walking on ice is available in Dezutter (1974).

9. Pattens are mentioned in line 1086 of *The Court of Love*; Forni (2005) glosses "patens" as "wooden clogs" in her edition of the poem.

10. The entire description of the Princess of Orange in the anonymous English translation cited by Fowler is as follows:

> It looked also as if the Prince of Orange's temper was altered, or that he had some impenetrable design, for he, who is so jealous that he does not permit his Princess to receive any private visit, not only from men, but women, presses the Duke of Monmouth to go after dinner to her, to teach her country-dances. They even made her act in characters which are unsuitable to a Princess, and which I should term ridiculous in an ordinary woman: for, in the great frost, which happened this year [1685], the Prince of Orange obliged her (such is her complaisance to him) to learn to skate upon the ice, because the Duke of Monmouth was also desirous of learning it. Twas a very extraordinary thing to see the Princess of Orange, with very short petticoats, and those tucked up half way to her waist, and with iron pattins on her feet, learning to slide, sometimes on one foot, sometimes on the other. (d'Avaux, 1755:III.132)

That the Princess's skating is described as "ridiculous

in an ordinary woman" shows that the later insistence on the suitability of skating for women was a significant change in attitude. Robert Jones saw "no reason why the ladies are to be excluded" and argued for their inclusion in the earliest extant book on skating (Thurber, 2017:25–26).

11. Olaf Goubitz argues that pattens with spikes on the bottom for walking on ice provided the inspiration for metal-bladed skates (Goubitz et al., 2001:252). Mulder (2008a,b) takes this idea further and describes how metal-bladed skates may have evolved from pattens and bone skates.

12. Johan Wolfgang von Goethe (1749–1832) describes himself as a "leidenschaftliche Schlittschuhfahrer" (passionate skater) in his autobiography, *Aus meinem Leben: Dichtung und Wahrheit (From my Life: Poetry and Truth)* (Trunz, 1948:61). He describes the etymological part of his conversation with Klopstock as follows:

> We spoke namely in good southern German of *Schlittschuhen*, which he did not accept as valid because the the word does not come from *Schlitten*, as if one puts on little runners, but rather from *Schreiten*, that is, one, like the Homeric gods, strides over the sea become a floor on winged shoes. (Trunz, 1948:III.61–62)

The autobiography goes on to include Klopstock's recommendations for skates (he prefers the long Frisian type). More details of Goethe's passion for ice skating can be found in Gassner (1990).

Kluge and Seebold (2002:811) summarize current thinking on the history of *Schlittschuh*: it is the descendant of *Schrittschuh*, a compound formed from *schreiten* (to stride) and *Schuh* (shoe) that referred to any shoe suitable for taking large steps until the seventeenth century, when it began to refer to ice skates and became *Schlittschuh*. It is also interesting to note that in Germanic, the ancestor of *schreiten* actually referred to any smooth motion, not just sliding (see Thurber (2013) for a discussion of this word in Old Norse literature).

Schrittschuh first appears in a tenth-century manuscript of the *Aeneid*, where it glosses *talaria*, the word for Mercury's winged sandals (Madan, 1877:99). The manuscript in question is Auct. F. 1. 16 in the Bodleian Library at Oxford University, and the gloss (*scridscos*) is on folio 126b. In a variety of spellings, *Schrittschuh* continues to appear in medieval German literature. It glosses *petasum* in the Old High German *Summarium Heinrici*, an eleventh-century glossary, and *alatum calceamentum* (winged shoe) in other manuscripts (for a list, see Schützeichel (2004:VIII.394–395)).

Looking up *petasum* in a Latin dictionary shows that it refers to a type of hat, but medieval Germans thought it was a magical shoe. Notker explains this quite clearly in his eleventh-century commentary on Marcianus Capella's *De nuptiis philologiae et Mercurii (The Marriage of Philology and Mercury)*:

Petasum héizent greci singulariter alatum

> calciamentum mercurii. (Piper, 1882:I.701) (*Petasum* means, particularly to the Greeks, the winged shoe of Mercury.)

In Middle High German literature, *Schrittschuh* took on a life of its own. Meister Eckhart (c. 1260–c. 1328) describes mystical *Schrittschuhe* that would enable his listeners' souls to reach God in his *Sermo de tempore (Sermon on Time).* (Strauch, 1919:38.22–29).

13. The *Orbis sensualium pictus (Visible World in Pictures)* was originally written to help German-speaking children learn Latin.

14. The Swedish word *skridskor*, used for metal-bladed skates, contrasts with *isläggor*, which refers specifically to bone skates (Sahlstedt, 1773:495, 251).

15. For a more recent English translation of FitzStephen's *Description of London*, see Douglas and Greenaway (1968:956–962) The Latin is available in Robertson (1877).

16. Although archaeologists have occasionally suggested that bone points were used with skating poles (see, e.g., Lauwerier and Van Heeringen (1998)), metal points seem to have been the norm.

17. The image Fowler objects to so strongly, from Smith (1848:167), is shown in figure C2.

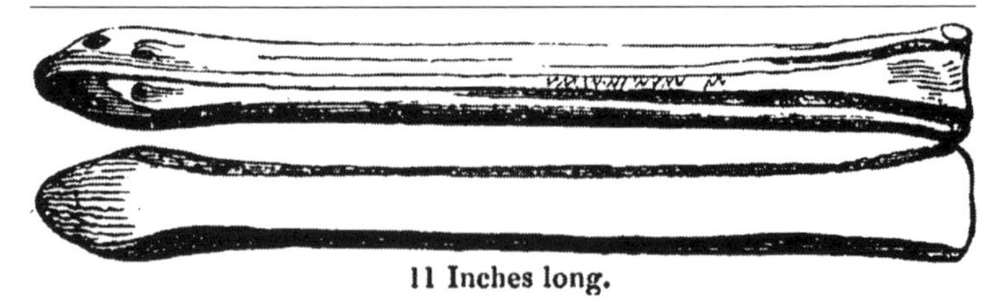

Figure C2: The woodcut of a bone skate that Fowler objects to.

18. The drawings of bone skates that Fowler approves of, from Heathcote (1892:5) and Munro (1894:186), are shown in figures C3 and C4, respectively. Identifying bone skates in the archaeological record remains difficult and occasionally controversial. See, for example, MacGregor (1975).

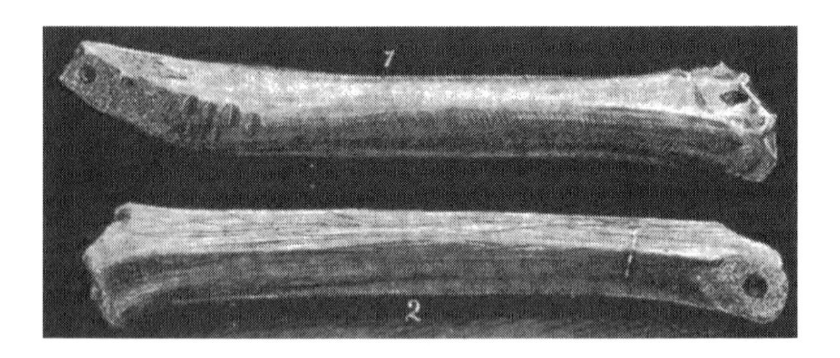

Figure C3: The bone skate from the Badminton Library's volume on skating that Fowler approves of.

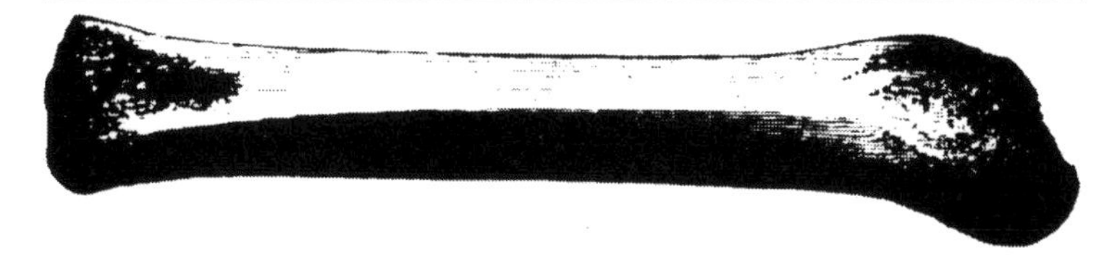

Figure C4: The bone skate from Munro (1894:186) that Fowler approves of.

19. Virchow (1870) describes his *Piekschlitten* as the simplest type; in a later article, Virchow (1887), he describes another type of *Piekschlitten* and includes a drawing (Figure C5). A significant difference between this sled and the type described by Fowler is that the latter sled is made from a jawbone rather than a board and leg bones. A small child would have been able to sit on the board and move by pushing with one or two poles. Mandibular sleds such as this are shown in paintings by Pieter Bruegel the Elder (*The St. George Gate at Antwerp* (1555) and *Adoration of the Magi* (1557)). Leg bones were also used for sled runners in the manner Fowler describes; in fact, sleds based on them may have been more common than mandibular sleds. Such bone runners look very similar to bone skates, but they can be easily identified by holes running vertically through the bone as it sits on the ice. In contrast, the holes in bone skates are horizontal or axial, if there are any. For a full discussion of bone sled runners, see MacGregor (1985:144–146).

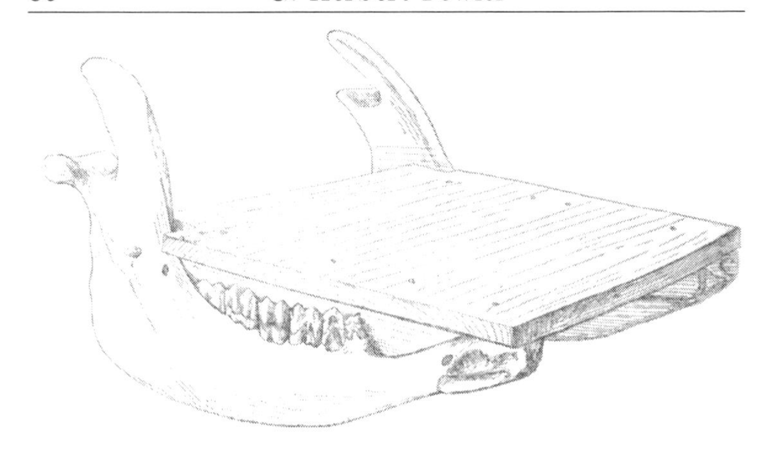

Figure C5: Virchow's mandibular sled.

20. Lewis (1895:8) states that

> the ancestor of the skate was not the sandal of the South, but the snow shoe, or the skid or skee of the North. Some writers have contended, that skids with iron runners, and thus skates in effect, were used in Northern Europe as far back as the year 200, but the contention is based on enthusiasm rather than evidence.

This may be the "recent manual of skating" Fowler is referring to.

21. The National Skating Palace was an artificially frozen rink built in London in the mid-1890s. The 1898 World Championship was held there. The site now hosts the London Palladium (Richardson, 1956:32).

22. It is now clear that bone skates were used for skating with poles in the manner described by FitzStephen. Pushing with the toe, as Fowler was able to do, requires the skates to be attached to the skater's feet, which was not always the case—many bone skates lack holes for attachment.

23. For a modern English translation of this passage, see Fisher and Higgens (1996:57–58).

24. Henry Balfour compares bone skates and what he calls "runner-skates" in Balfour (1898). His argument is similar to Fowler's.

25. The Norwegian speed and figure skater Axel Paulsen (1855–1938) is best known for the one-and-a-half-revolution jump that bears his name. He first performed this jump at an international competition in 1882 (Hines, 2011:177).

26. The phrase *evolutio per saltum* means "evolution through a jump," i.e., discontinuous evolution.

27. There is no evidence for the "tradition" that modern skates were the result of a mistake.

28. There are far more than eight woodcuts in Olaus Magnus's 1555 *Historia de gentibus septentrionalibus (Description of the Northern Peoples)*, but most show neither skating nor skiing. The woodcut that best represents both is shown in figure C6.

Figure C6: Skaters and skiers from Olaus Magnus's *Historia de gentibus septentrionalibus (Description of the Northern Peoples)* (1555).

29. Eighteenth- and nineteenth-century mistranslations of medieval Scandinavian literature are still occasionally cited in the twenty-first century. Old Norse poetry comes in two main types, eddic and skaldic. The latter is the type that appears in the sagas, and it is notoriously difficult to translate. Some early translators avoided this task by simply replacing the poems with vaguely related poems of their own. One example is Samuel Liang's version of a poem from *Haralds saga Gráfeldar (The Saga of Harald Greycloak)* in Snorri Sturluson's *Heimskringla*, which dates to c. 1230 (Liang, 1844). His poem reads

> I go across the ocean-foam,
> Swift skating to my Iceland home
> Upon the ocean-skates, fast driven
> By gales by Thurse's witch fire given.
> For from the falcon-bearing hand
> Harald has plucked the gold snake band
> My father wore—by lawless might
> Has taken what is mine by right.

A more accurate translation of the Old Norse poem is that of Hollander (1964:131):

> Should I, ship's keen steerer,
> share thy favor henceforth:
> would that well befit thee,
> warrior, ruling Norway,
> seeing I give thee this goodly
> golden arm ring, dragon's-
> lair's rich treasure, liege,
> which long had owned my father.

Liang's translation highlights two problems with early translations of the sagas: first, that the enthusiasm of the translators led them to put skating where it should not be, and second, that the meaning of the word "skate" has become more specific over time. Before "ski" became common in English, skis were called "skates" or "snowshoes." Since this is no longer the case, older texts can be confusing to modern readers. The word that may have inspired Liang's use of "skating" and "ocean-skates" is *skíðrennandi*, which literally means "ski-running." In skaldic verse, "skis of the sea" and similar phrases were used as kennings for ships, and the verb *skríða* was used for the smooth gliding motions of ships and skiers. Details of these issues can be found in Thurber (2013).

30. The Danish archaeologist Jens Jacob Asmussen Worsaae (1821–1885) is best known for showing how the Three-Age System (Stone, Bronze, and Iron) related to stratigraphy at archaeological sites (Fagan, 1996).

31. The saga in question here, *Magnússona saga (The Saga of the Sons of Magnus)*, is one of the sagas in *Heimskringla.* Hollander (1964) provides a modern translation. This saga contains the only instance of the Old Norse word *ísleggir* in the corpus, but may not be the only reference to skating: *Hávamal*, one of the poems of the *Poetic Edda*, includes the verse *Við eld skal ǫl drekka // en á ísi skríða* (Dronke, 2011:III.18) (Drink ale by a fire, slide when on ice), which could refer to skating, and *Fljótsdœla saga* includes an episode in which a character uses *beinspýtum* to travel over a frozen river (Jón Johánnesson, 1950:250). Halldór Halldórsson (1956) argues that these are bone skates, and this interpretation has been tentatively accepted by the editors of the newest Old Norse dictionary, Degnbol et al. (2010). For details of bone skates in Old Norse literature, see Thurber (2013).

32. Saxo Grammaticus's *Gesta danorum (History of the Danes)* was written in the twelfth century; for a modern translation of the first nine books, see Davidson and Fisher (1980).

33. Olaus Magnus retells this story and includes a woodcut that depicts Ullr (or Holler, as Olaus Magnus calls him) crossing the sea on what appears to be a surfboard (Fisher and Higgens (1996:176); see figure C7). It is generally thought to be a bone skate. No bone skates with spells engraved on them have emerged from the archaeological record yet, but Edberg and Karlsson (2015:fig. 21) shows a decorated skate from Birka.

Figure C7: Holler on his magic bone, which looks like a surfboard, from Olaus Magnus's *Historia de gentibus septentrionalibus (Description of the Northern Peoples)* (1555).

34. The woodcut of St. Lÿdwine's accident is shown in

figure C8. This is often described as the first picture of skating, but there is an earlier depiction of metal-bladed skates on the verso of folio 1a of manuscript Douce 5 in the Bodleian Library at Oxford University. The lower right corner of the page for February in the calendar of St. Pierre of Blandigny near Ghent shows a person skating without a pole on what must have been metal-bladed skates. This image, which dates to between AD 1320 and 1330 according to its page in the Oxford Digital Library, is published in Randall (1966:31, no. 471) and has been cited by Blauw (2001:11), Küchelmann and Zidarov (2005:432), and Mulder (2009a:27). A high-resolution, full-color version is available online in the Oxford Digital Library. The earliest metal-bladed skates that have been found so far date to approximately AD 1225 (Goubitz, 2000).

35. The "deliciously graphic" Latin text means

> Look! One of the girls, coming toward her on a rapid course and, unable to stop the course due to the impetus, crashed into Lÿdwine casually and, having been struck, she fell down on broken ice in an awful collision and in this way, having fallen, she caused one rib to be broken inward.

For a modern edition of Brugman's Latin text, see de Meyer (1963). For more information on St. Lÿdwine in English, Huysmans (1923) is a modern biography that is available in English translation.

Figure C8: The famous woodcut of St. Lÿdwine's accident.

36. Saint Lÿdwine's name has been spelled in many different ways, including Lydwine, Lydwina, Lidwina, Lidwine, Lijdwine, and Liedewij. For consistency with Fowler's convention, she is referred to as "Lÿdwine" throughout this book.

37. The Middle Dutch life of St. Lÿdwine says "ghinc si op scholoedsen" (Jongen and Schotel, 1994:24). This means "she went on *scholoedsen*." What are *scholoedsen*? They are usually considered skates in this context because of the famous woodcut from Johannes

Brugman's retelling of the *Life* (figure C8), but generally, they are clogs with leather uppers or pattens (Verwijs et al., 90 :s.v. "schalootse"). Mulder (2009b:38) suggests that Lÿdwine was walking on ice in such shoes, possibly with spikes attached to the bottom for traction, when she fell. This means that the patron saint of skating may not have been a skater after all.

38. The "recent manual" Fowler refers to may be Hoffman (1897:373). The idea that Dutch prisoners brought metal-bladed skates to England during Cromwell's time (1599–1658) goes back to at least the 1850s (Urban, 1853:31) and is still occasionally cited despite the lack of verification. The date seems reasonable since the earliest known references to skating in London are the December 1, 1662, diary entries of Samuel Pepys and John Evelyn (see Thurber (2017:4)). The idea that Dutch prisoners were responsible for skating seems less likely because metal-bladed skates seem to have been used by gentlemen at first; people living in rural areas continued using bone skates well into the twentieth century.

39. Rev. Jonathan Swift (1667–1745) mentions skates in a letter to Stella (Esther Johnson, 1681–1728) written in London on January 31, 1711 (Nichols, 1801:341–342).

40. The simplest effective way to attach bone skates is the left-hand one in figure C9. Fowler's method is conceptually similar but relies on a second lace through

the heel of the skate instead of using a single lace. The lack of a lace around the skater's heel may have made Fowler's method less stable.

Figure C9: Methods of tying bone skates to the feet described by Herman (1902:220).

41. Fowler's interpretation of this picture is a bit off. It is now generally thought to depict a person on bone skates, not the shod clogs Fowler mentions, though Fowler's interpretation is understandable because the skates do not look like bone skates at all. This discrepancy can probably be attributed to the artist's lack of knowledge about bone skates; skis look very similar (see figure C6). Olaus Magnus is unlikely to have included a depiction of metal-bladed because he considers them inferior to bone skates. He notes that people on bone skates regularly win races because bone has less friction against ice than iron does (Fisher and Higgens,

1996:58). His suppositions about the friction were confirmed by Formenti and Minetti (2007), who found that replicas of thirteenth-century metal-bladed skates had a higher coefficient of friction than bone skates. The real advantage of metal-bladed skates comes from foot-pushing, which Olaus Magnus seems not to have known about.

42. Romeyn de Hooghe (1645–1708) was a prolific Dutch artist.

43. The "toe spike" is not the same as the toe pick on modern figure skate blades. The toe pick is the set of teeth at the front of the blade that skaters use for jumping. Careful examination of the figures reveals that these skates have no toe picks. Fowler is probably referring to the upward curl at the front of the blade, which becomes substantially smaller between figures 7 and 8.

The "curvature of the blade's edge" probably refers to the rocker radius, which is the curvature of the blade from front to back. Modern figure skate blades typically have a radius of curvature of seven or eight feet, depending on the model.

44. This is still said today; Hines (2006:49) reports that Peter the Great attached blades to his boots in 1697. I have been unable to verify this assertion. It is possible; Peter the Great spent about five months in Amsterdam in 1678 studying shipbuilding before departing in early January 1679 (Massie, 1980:202). Massie (1980:189) reports, without citing a source, that Peter saw people

skating; the lack of a source indicates that this statement may be to add color to his account of Peter's visit instead of being supported by data. But overall, the picture Massie (1980:155–202) paints of Peter in the Netherlands is one of a man who was interested in learning as much has he could about making things. This is consistent with the idea of him making new skates. In contrast, Peter's departure in early January gives him little time for skating. Fagan (2000:113) describes the half-century between 1680 and 1730 as extremely cold, which implies that Peter probably had the opportunity to skate, but there is always substantial variability on a year-to-year basis. Peter's January departure suggests that the weather was not too bad.

45. Combined figures are concerned with the geometric precision of movements made by a group of skaters (usually four). Sometimes they are managed by a caller, who announces the movements to be performed by the group in a way that is reminiscent of square dancing. Combined skating shares some features with synchronized skating, but is perhaps closest to the Pattern Team event in competitions run by ISI (Ice Skating Institute, recently renamed Ice Sports Industry) member facilities (Ice Skating Institute, 2012:193), but without music. Details can be found in many of the old skating manuals; Hines (2008) is a good starting point for modern readers. Vandervell and Witham (1880) provide more details, and a comprehensive list can be found in Monier-Williams and Monier-Williams (1883).

46. *Encyclopædia Perthensis* puts the formation of the

Edinburgh Skating Club "about 50 years ago" or in about 1766 (Anonymous, 1816:26). *Encyclopædia Metropolitana* puts it "in or about the year 1760" (Smedley et al., 1845:848). Hines (2006:27) discusses the same issues Fowler does and concludes that "[t]he club could date from later in the seventeenth century, sometime after the Restoration, but was probably not formed before the second quarter of the eighteenth century." A date in the 1760s, as suggested by both encyclopedias, seems reasonable.

47. The final chapter of *Frostiana*, a charming little book whose title page was printed on the Thames during the Great Frost of 1813–1814, is about skating and includes the suggestion that, when learning the outside edge, "much assistance may be derived from placing *a bag of lead-shot* in the pocket next to the *foot employed in making the outside stroke*, which will produce an artificial poise of the body; this afterwards will become natural by practice" (Anonymous, 1814:120). It also includes the following instructions for making ice cream:

> Ice cream is prepared by mixing three parts of cream with one part of the juice or jam of raspberries, currants, &c. The mixture is then well beaten; and, after being strained through a cloth, is poured into a pewter mould or vessel, adding a small quantity of lemon-juice. The mould is now covered, and plunged in a pail about two thirds full of ice, into which two handfuls of salt should be previously scattered. The vessel containing

> the cream is then briskly agitated for eight or ten minutes, after which it is suffered to stand for a similar space of time; the agitation is then repeated, and the cream allowed to subside for half an hour, when it is taken out of the mould, and sent to table. (Anonymous, 1814:70–71)

This book contains many other bits of advice, some better than others, including instructions for making a flotation device from a top hat and handkerchief that enables a non-swimmer to save someone who is drowning (Anonymous, 1814:74–76).

48. Vandervell and Witham (1880:164–166) describe the figure "two turns" as follows:

> The old name of half-double gives perhaps a false idea of its nature; it is not the half of the well-known double 3, and it must not be confounded with it. When applied to the cross movements, it forms an alternating combination exceedingly curious and graceful, and by many preferred to the double 3 proper.
>
> *Two Turns A.*—One turn from the inside forwards, which places the skater on the outside backwards, from which another turn is made, restoring him again to the inside forwards. [...] *Two Turns C.*—One from the outside forwards, which places him

> on the inside backwards, from which another turn is made, restoring him again to the outside forwards.

This sounds just like a modern double 3, but in the nineteenth century, a double 3 actually consisted of three 3s: Vandervell and Witham (1880:167) note that a double 3 "is effected by adding one more turn to the last figure."

49. In the nineteenth century, a double 3 consisted of three 3s in a row. It had the same effect as a single 3—it changed the direction of the skater's motion from forward to backward or vice versa—but used multiple turns. Vandervell and Witham (1880:168) note that

> [t]o skate the double 3 to perfection, an immense amount of hard practice is necessary; it will not yield to a bungler. To make a few hurried spins, the whole of which can be surrounded by a child's hoop perhaps, and fancy we are doing the double 3, is a great delusion, and, as a rule, the performer who so makes them can only do them at a happy moment, and as often fails in his attempts as not.

50. Vandervell and Witham (1880:184–186) describe a Q as follows:

> The Q figure is extremely simple; it is nothing more than an opposite curve, placed before or after a turn. The curve placed before

> the turn gives four varieties, as does also the curve placed after the turn. Simple as the addition is, it is no trifle in practice. [...]
>
> Q C is begun with a curve of outside forwards, and, when some distance has been traversed, a change of edge is effected, by leaning over to inside forwards, on which Turn A is made, and the resulting curve of outside backwards continued until the circle or body of the Q is complete.

Turn A is an inside forward 3. A Q can be started on any edge and always consists of a change of edge and a 3. The exit edge is held for a full circle.

51. A reverse Q is simply a Q done in reverse, i.e., starting with the circle and ending with the change of edge. Vandervell and Witham (1880:195) describe "Reverse Q C" as follows:

> Reverse Q C is begun by describing a whole circle of outside forwards, when Turn C is immediately made, and the resulting curve of inside backwards continued for a short distance. The change of edge is then effected by leaning over to outside backwards, which completes the figure.

Turn C is an outside forward 3.

52. *A System of Figure Skating* by Henry Eugene Vandervell and T. Maxwell Witham was, as Fowler notes, a monumental achievement and remains the most thorough description of English-style skating available. It

went through several editions by both authors (1869, 1874, 1880, and 1889) plus two more (1893, 1897) by Witham alone.

53. *The Field* is a newspaper published in London for much of the nineteenth century, through the twentieth, and into the twenty-first. It focused on topics of interest to upper-class men with country estates. Winter issues featured regular columns on skating during the nineteenth century.

54. Grapevines are long, intricate figures skated on two feet. Some nineteenth-century skaters did not consider them worth doing because real skating was supposed to be done on only one foot at a time. Vandervell and Witham (1880:205) recognize their charm with the following:

> Although it will have become apparent to our readers that we are great advocates for pure skating, as exemplified by long-sustained efforts on one or the other foot, yet it would be absurd to ignore the beauties of the two-footed figures which are known to most figure-skaters as "the grape-vines."

The first edition of their book, Vandervell and Witham (1869:259) note the existence of these figures ("There are several Canadian and American two-footed figures, such as the 'Grape Vine'...") without attempting to describe them or even suggest that they might be worthwhile. Grapevines were relatively short-lived in figure skating—they are no longer skated today—but look like they could be the basis for many of the tricks done in freestyle slalom skating.

55. Cross-cuts are like loops, but flat across the top with turns at the corners; they look like fish. Often, skaters make them by accident while learning loops. Cupid's bow is essentially a cross-cut in which the two sides of the loop are pulled apart. A full discussion can be found in Vandervell and Witham (1880:178–183).

56. Witham's essay in *Badminton Magazine* is quite interesting for its description of skating and predictions for what was to come. Witham predicted that although the ability to skate year-round (on ice or roller skates) and indoor ice rinks provide

> the opportunity of continuous practice, the space available is contracted and crowded, and the chances are that, from an English point of view, the skating will deteriorate. Individual acrobatic performances on skates will doubtless develop enormously, but the accuracy and correct pose which have hitherto distinguished English skating, as seen to perfection in the 'Club figures,' will be lost. (Witham, 1895:612)

This seems quite accurate.

57. The "early Encyclopaedia" was probably Valentin Trichter's *Curiöses Reit- Jagd- Fecht- Tanz- oder Ritter-Exercitien Lexicon (Lexicon of Curious Riding, Hunt-*

ing, Dancing, or Knightly Exercises) (1742), which includes the following information under "Schritt-Schuhe" (ice skates):

> They are certain flattened irons that people bind under their feet in winter in many places, especially in Holland, and with them travel back and forth quickly across the frozen ice. This is considered a type of bodily exercise, but is often dangerous. Even dames in Holland use it to show their artistic routes. (Trichter, 1742:2083)

58. The loop 3 may be the figure described in the following passage from Vieth (1789:124):

> I skip over some artificialities that one can make with skates, in part because practicising them is sometimes unadvisable because of the danger associated with some of them and in part because they are never as beautiful as the spiral motion. Among the best of these is, for example, the figure of a written Latin E. A glance easily shows what violent motion the tight curvature of the middle requires if enough power is to remain for the final curve.

59. Jackson Haines (1840–1875), whose last name was frequently spelled Haynes in the nineteenth century, is often credited with originating modern figure skating

by bringing dance to the ice. Hines (2006:51–53) provides an overview of his life and contributions. The "essentially American" movements probably included grapevines and spins. Haines has been credited with inventing the sit spin (Hines, 2011:107).

60. Once back is one of the easier combined figures skated in the English style. Vandervell and Witham (1880:226) describe it as follows:

> This is commenced by a 3 on right, then the left foot down for outside back for some distance, then another 3 on right, which has the effect generally of bringing each skater nearly the quarter of the circle past the starting-place of his partner, that is (supposing four are skating) almost into the original starting-place of his left-hand neighbour.

61. The only candidate for an important book about skating published in Germany in 1880 listed in Foster (1898) is ten Brink (1880).

62. Joseph Bologne, Chevalier de Saint-Georges (as his name is usually spelled now) was born in Guadaloupe to a planter and a slave. He spent most of his life in France, where he was known as an accomplished fencer and violinist as well as an excellent skater. He is thought to be the first black composer of classical music in Europe. More information about his life can be found in Banat (2006).

63. There is now a copy of *Le Vrai Patineur (The True Skater)* in the National Art Library in the Victoria and Albert Museum in London, but it may not have been there in Fowler's time.

64. Vandervell and Witham (1880:286) quote the following description of "On to Richmond" (also called the Back Scratch) from *The Skater's Text-book*:

> In executing the movement the skater is apparently endeavouring to go forward, but in reality goes backward.
>
> Stand with the left foot straight, and lifting the right foot clear of the ice, hoisting the toe of the foot to its greatest possible extent. In this position cross it over in front of and as far across the left as possible, at the same time allowing the weight of the body to fall upon the outside edge of the right foot. Raise the left foot, turning the toe out; cross it over in front of the right, allowing the weight of the body to come upon the outside edge of the left foot.

65. The book by Paulin-Désormeaux was probably published in 1853, not 1854.

66. Benoît Baudouin's book *De calceo antiquo (On Ancient Shoes)*, first published in 1615 under the Latinized version of his name, *Balduinus*, is quite interesting for the study of early shoes. It includes a picture of a skier

(figure C10) on skis that are quite similar to the ones in Olaus Magnus's woodcuts (compare figure C6), a drawing of a skate tied on in a manner similar to one of those described by Herman (1902:220) (see figure C9), and a more accurate drawing of a ski. The latter drawings are shown in figure C11. The description of skates is in a footnote:

> And the last type of narta [ski], I think, is the *Calopodia*, with which the Dutch playfully wander when the water is covered in ice as quickly as possible in all directions. The people call them *Schaatsen* (skates), a most excellent vehicle, but one that requires a trained person. (Balduinus and Nigronus, 1667:40)

67. The description of skating in Holland in 1788 in the *Gothaischer Hof Kalender (Gotha's Court Almanac)* (Anonymous, 1788) is not long. It is as follows:

> Skating
>
> The masters of skating are the people living in the provinces of Holland, Friesland and Utrecht. Often such a skater leaves for a period of one hour and returns in three or four. This physical exercise, which is rightfully known as one of the strongest and hardest and which the people from England, when they are in Holland, prefer to all other winter recreations, was adopted

Figure C10: The skier from Balduinus's *De calceo antiquo (On Ancient Shoes)* (1667).

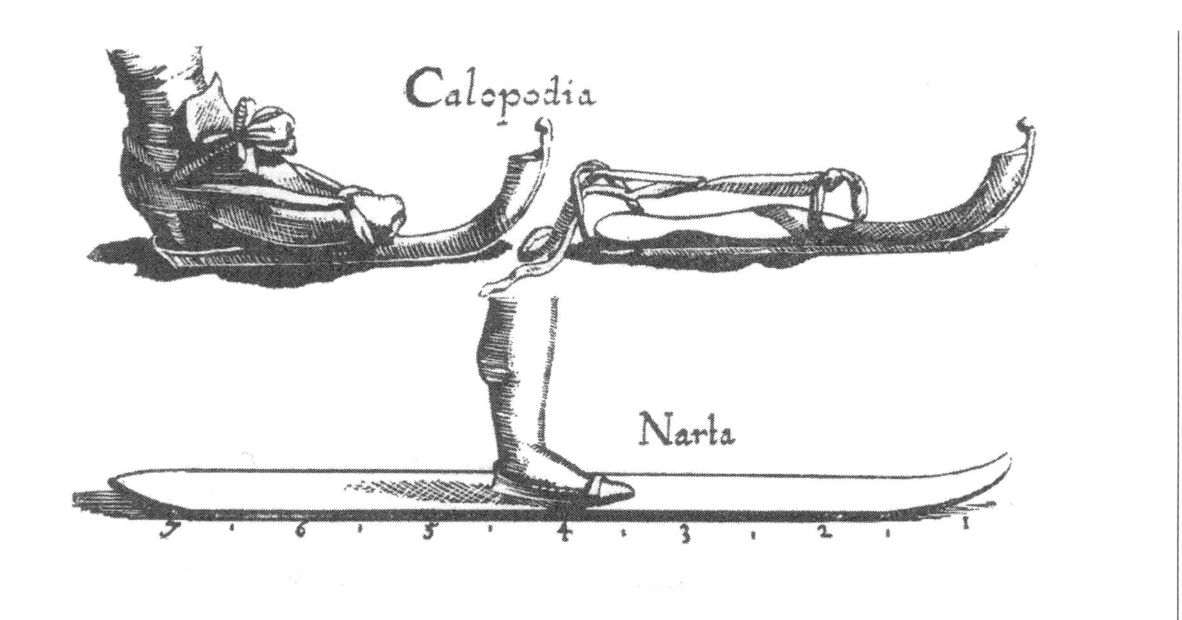

Figure C11: The skate and ski from Balduinus's *De calceo antiquo* (*On Ancient Shoes*) (1667).

from the people of the farthest North, who travel through their snow-filled [homelands] on wooden skates, for example, the Laplanders and the Kamchadals, the Nenets, and the inhabitants of Canada, by the Dutch, as Balduin explains. The Dutch, especially the inhabitants of Waterland, Delft, and Rheinland and the mariners of Korwyck, can be identified by the ease and grace with which they lean their bodies to the side as they hold themselves upright. There are some who, with every push or stroke, complete a part of a circle of 3 or 4 Toise [approximately 18–24 feet]; others engrave intricate names and similar symbols into the ice with the end of the skate. The Frisians do not love such tricks; they are content with moving themselves straight and are also very firm on the ice and, in a given time, return most of the way.

By the middle of this century, elegant Dutch women were very skilled skaters. The ice was covered with people of both genders. On a meadow that had been flooded and covered with a thick crust of ice, an upper-class woman could often be seen skating between two farmers, or a young man of standing with a farmer girl on his arm. It was a prime mark of favor to put on a lady's skates, and she rewarded this labor on the job with a kiss. Later, this familiarity stopped, and the Dutch nobility began to be untrue to this old custom. However, there remain many ladies who love this fun; also, all the farmer girls and country-dwellers go on skates.

One often sees thirty people behind one another, namely, fifteen young fellows, each with his girl, holding hands. The expert and most skilled are at the front or the end of the line, the weaker ones are placed in the middle. In this way, the inexperienced are pulled along by the others, and this long row develops a regular motion and is a pleasant sight. This group does not stop until it reaches a designated place. Then, the leader describes a half circle, with all the followers doing the same. If one lets go of the hand of his neighbor, he usually loses his balance and entangles all the others in his fall.

To allow children and dames to participate in the pleasures of travel on ice, small blades that stand on long irons that are bent in front instead of runners have been devised. The husband or lover stands on skates behind such a sled, which fits one or two people comfortably, and pushes it quickly in front of himself. There are also barges, 10–15 feet long, that feature masts and large sails and run on large skates. The speed of these skate-barges, when the wind

> fills their spread sails, exceeds all expectations; they seem to fly over the ice; in less than a quarter of an hour a mile lies behind, and often a quarter hour in two minutes. Travelling in these barges is dangerous in itself and often causes dangerous illnesses and accidents due to the great speed that takes away the breath.

The description of 30 people skating together may be the first appearance of synchronized skating.

68. The book by van Geuns cited by Fowler is probably his translation (from German to Dutch) of Gutsmuths (1793). Gutsmuths was well-known for developing the idea of physical education, and his collection of exercises for young people includes a short section on skating.

69. *Deutscher Eissport* (German Ice-Sport) was the journal of the Deutsche Eislauf Verband (German Skating Federation), the organization that governed skating and other ice sports in Germany and nearby countries.

70. According to OCLC Worldcat, the only book with the title *Das Schlittschuhfahren (Skating)* published in 1827 is by Franz Gräffer, not F. E. Fergar, who is listed as the author in Foster (1898:40). The book's entry in Kayser (1834:204) shows that F. E. Fergar was a pseudonym used by Franz Gräffer. Unfortunately, very few copies have survived.

71. *Spuren auf dem Eise (Tracings on the Ice)* is a monumental work that classifies all the known figures systematically, including special figures. It was a standard reference work for skaters in the late nineteenth century. The following passage is probably what Fowler is referring to:

> It was in winter 1864–1865 that one of these North American skaters, Jackson Haynes, first came over the ocean and presented public performances in many cities in Northern Europe. They were met with wonder, and from them people understood, that the motherland had been surpassed by the daughter. The first skaters in Europe recognized Haynes as their master. The appearance of Haynes was a deciding point in favor of artistic skating, and the young people were nowhere so eager to follow his example than the skaters of Vienna. Today, there are some who have not only equaled the master in strength and beauty but also overtaken him in overcoming difficult evolutions and in completing the school, so that now, Vienna, with its splendidly organized skating club, rivals New York in the ice sport. (Diamantidi et al., 1892:15–16)

72. Fowler's citation of the 1868 Swedish book on skating is slightly incorrect, which makes the book difficult

to track down. The author is actually Falck Ytter (not Ytta), and the correct title is *Kroppsöfningar och lekar (Physical Exercises and Games)* (Ytter, 1868).

73. Fowler's citation of the Danish book on skating is not quite right; the correct title is *Skøteløberkunsten eller Anviisning til Skøiteløbning saavel for Begyndere som Viderekomne (The Art of Skating or Advice on Skating for both Beginners and Advanced* (Høegh-Guldberg, 1867).

74. Hines (2006:53) reports that Haines died in Finland in 1875.

Further reading

A good introduction to current thinking on bone skates is Küchelmann and Zidarov (2005), which is available on Hans Christian Küchelmann's website.* This site also includes a searchable database of several thousand bone skates. Those who can read Dutch will find *Kouwe Drukte*† a cornucopia of information about early metal-bladed skates and their evolution into modern speed skates. Of particular interest are Niko Mulder's articles about skates from the pioneer stage (Mulder, 2008b,a, 2009b, 2010). Blauw (2001) and Schaatshistorie.nl‡ are other great resources for studying the evolution of skates. Those who can't read Dutch should learn. There simply isn't very much about early metal-bladed skates available in English.

For an introduction to medieval Scandinavian studies, a good choice is Jesse Byock's *Viking Language I*, which introduces Old Norse grammar and vocabulary alongside medieval Icelandic culture. Those interested in history may prefer to begin with one of the many popular introductions to the subject, such as Anders Winroth's *Age of the Vikings*. *The Sagas of Icelanders*, edited by Jane Smiley, provides a good selection of Icelandic sagas in translation (but not the ones that mention skating).

---

*http://www.knochenarbeit.de/en/index.php?-page=bone_skates

†http://www.verzamelkringdepoolster.nl/kouwe-drukte/

‡http://www.schaatshistorie.nl/

English-style skating in the nineteenth century is aptly covered by Henry Eugene Vandervell and T. Maxwell Witham in the various editions of *A System of Figure Skating*; I have mostly referenced the third edition (Vandervell and Witham, 1880) because it contains details of more figures than earlier editions and is nearly the last (the last being the revised third edition of 1889) to include Henry Vandervell as an author. James Hines's book on the history and survival of English style skating, Hines (2008), which seems to only be available from Lulu,* is a nice introduction to the subject for modern skaters without the background assumed by Vandervell and Witham. For skating on the continent toward the end of the nineteenth century, the biggest and best book is *Spuren auf dem Eise (Tracings on the Ice)*, published in 1881 with an expanded second edition in 1892. It is only available in German.

For an overall view of the evolution of figure skating, read *Artistic Impressions* by Mary Louise Adams. Adams (2011) explains how figure skating evolved from a pastime for adult men to a sport whose participants are predominantly young girls.

*http://www.lulu.com/

References

Adams, M. L.
2011. *Artistic Impressions: Figure Skating, Masculinity, and the Limits of Sport.* Toronto: University of Toronto Press.

Anderson, G.
1868. *The Art of Skating: Containing Many Figures Never Previously Described.* London: Horace Cox.

Anonymous
1788. Das Schlittschuh-Laufen. In *Gothaischer Hof Kalender zum Nutzen und Vergnügen eingerichtet auf das Jahr 1788*, pp. 87–88. Gotha: C. W. Ettinger.

Anonymous
1814. *Frostiana: Or a History of the River Thames in a Frozen State; with an Account of the Late Severe Frost; and the Wonderful Effects of Frost, Snow, Ice, and Cold, in England, and in Different Parts of the World; Interspersed with Various Amusing Anecdotes. To Which is Added, the Art of Skating.* London: G. Davis.

Anonymous
1816. *Encyclopædia Perthensis; or Universal Dictionary of the Arts, Sciences, Literature, etc., Inteneded to Supersede the Use of Other Books of Reference,* volume 21. Edinburgh: John Brown.

Anonymous
1861. Sketches from Pekin. *The Illustrated London News*, 38(1076):159, 171.

Anonymous
1862. *Physiologie du patineur, ou définition complète des principes et des règles qui s'appliquent à l'exercice du patin.* Paris: Dentu.

Anonymous
1869. *Les patins et l'art de patiner.* Paris: P. M. Laroche.

Anonymous
1898. Figure skating. *The Field*, 91(2349):121.

Balduinus, B. and J. Nigronus
1667. *De calceo antiquo et de caliga veterum.* Amsterdam: Andreas Frisius.

Balfour, H.
1898. Notes on the modern use of bone skates. *The Reliquary and Illustrated Archaeologist*, 4:29–37.

Banat, G.
2006. *The Chevalier de Saint-Georges: Virtuoso of the Sword and Bow*, volume 7 of *Lives in Music.* Hillsdale, NY: Pendragon Press.

Beaulieu, M. and J. Baylé
1956. *Le costume en Bourgogne de Philippe le Hardi à la mort de Charles le Téméraire (1364–1477).* Paris: Presses universitaires de France.

Bell, P. and F. Stitt
2002. George Herbert Fowler and county records. *Journal of the Society of Archivists*, 23(2):249–264. doi:10.1080/00379810220120618.

Bertolini, M. and U. T. Hohenstein
2016. Evidence of butchery marks and anthropic modifications on horse remains in a Late Bronze Age site of northern Italy: The case of Bovolone. *Journal of Archaeological Science: Reports*, 9:468–480. doi:10.1016/j.jasrep.2016.08.031.

Blauw, W.
2001. *Van glis tot klapschaats: Schaatsen en schaatsenmakers in Nederland, 1200 tot heden.* Franeker: Van Wijnen.

Brugman, J.
1498. *Vita alme virginis Lijdwine.* Schiedam: Otgier Nachtegael.

Byock, J.
2013. *Viking Language I.* Pacific Palisades, CA: Jules William Press.

Carr, W.
1688. *Remarks of the Government of Severall Parts of Germanie, Denmark, Sweedland, Hamburg, Lubeck, and Hansiatique Townes, but More Particularly of the United Provinces.* Amsterdam: n.p.

Choyke, A. M. and L. Bartosiewicz
2005. Skating with horses: Continuity and parallelism in prehistoric Hungary. *Revue de Paléobiologie*, spéc. 10:317–326.

Church of St. Augustine, Pendlebury, in the County of Lancashire
c. 2017. Marriages at St. Augustine in the District of Pendlebury, Salford: Marriages recorded in the register for the years 1874–1889. Online.

Clay, T.
1828. *Instructions on the Art of Skating, Containing Useful Lessons to Learners.* Leeds: Robinson, Hernamen and Wood.

Cleasby, R. and Gudbrand Vigfusson
1874. *An Icelandic-English Dictionary.* Oxford: Clarendon Press.

Comp., D. M.-S.
1897. *Geillustreerde catalogus van de Multiplex-Schaats.* Groningen: De Multiplex-Schaats Comp.

Cook, T. A., ed.
1909? *The Fourth Olympiad: Being the Official Report [of] The Olympic Games of 1908 Celebrated in London under the Patronage of His Most Gracious Majesty King Edward VII and by the Sanction of the International Olympic Committee.* London: The British Olympic Association.

Covilbeaux, A. P.
1842. *Patinotechnie ou manuel du patineur renfermant les vrais principes de l'art de patiner avec un système de classification des diverses poses et des figures.* Paris: Desloges.

Cyclos, J.
1852. *The Art of Skating with Plain Directions for the Acquirement of the Most Difficult and Elegant Maneuvers.* Glasgow: Thomas Murray and Son.

Cyclos, J.
1858. *Konsten att åka skridsko.* Söderhamn: n.p.

d'Avaux, C.
1754–1755. *The Negotiations of Count d'Avaux.* London: A. Millar, D. Wilson, and T. Durham.

Davidson, H. E. and P. Fisher, eds.
1980. *Saxo Grammaticus. The History of the Danes, Books I–IX.* Cambridge: D. S. Brewer.

de Mendoza, B.
1592. *Comentarios de Don Bernardino de Mendoça de lo sucedido en las Guerras de los Payses baxos, desde el año de 1567 hasta el de 1577.* Madrid: Pedro Madrigal.

de Meyer, A., ed.
1963. *Johannes Brugman. Vita alme virginis Liidwine*, volume 2 of *Teksten en documenten.* Groningen: J. B. Wolters.

Deacon, M. B.
1984. G. Herbert Fowler (1861–1940): The forgotten oceanographer. *Notes and Records of the Royal Society of London*, 38(2):261–296. doi:10.1098/rsnr.1984.0016.

Degnbol, H., B. C. Jacobsen, E. Rode, C. Sanders, and Þorbjörg Helgadóttir
2010. Ordbog over det norrøne prosasprog / A Dictionary of Old Norse Prose. Online.

Dezutter, W. P.
1974. Slijkschoenen: Twee aanwinsten voor het Stedelijk Museum voor Volkskunde te Brugge. *Biekorf*, 75:289–304.

Diamantidi, D., C. von Korper, and M. Wirth
1892. *Spuren auf dem Eise: Die Entwicklung des Eislaufes auf der Bahn des Wiener Eislauf-Vereines*, second edition. Vienna: Alfred Hölder.

Douglas, D. C. and G. W. Greenaway, eds.
1968. *English Historical Documents*, volume 2: 1042–1189. Oxford: Oxford University Press.

Dronke, U., ed.
1969–2011. *The Poetic Edda.* Oxford: Clarendon Press.

Edberg, R. and J. Karlsson
2015. *Isläggor från Birka och Sigtuna. En undersökning av ett vikingatida och medeltida fyndmate-*

rial, volume 43 of *Stockholm Archaeological Reports*. Stockholm: Institutionen för arkeologi och antikens kultur, Stockholms universitet.

Edberg, R. and J. Karlsson
2016. Bone skates and young people in Birka and Sigtuna. *Fornvännen*, 111:7–16.

Fagan, B.
2000. *The Little Ice Age: How Climate Made History 1300–1850*. New York: Basic Books.

Fagan, B. M.
1996. Worsaae, Jens Jacob Asmussen. In *The Oxford Companion to Archaeology*, B. M. Fagan, ed., p. 761. Oxford: Oxford University Press.

Fergar, F. E.
1827. *Das Schlittschuhfahren: Eine practische Anleitung zum schnellen und richtigen Selbsterlernen dieser genußvollen, stärkenden und edlen Kunst; nebst einigen Beygaben*. Vienna: Haas.

Fisher, P. and H. Higgens, eds.
1996. *Olaus Magnus. Description of the Northern Peoples*. London: The Hakluyt Society.

Formenti, F. and A. E. Minetti
2007. Human locomotion on ice: The evolution of ice-skating energetics through history. *Journal of Experimental Biology*, 210:1825–1833. doi:10.1242/jeb.002162.

Formenti, F. and A. E. Minetti
2008. The first humans travelling on ice: An energy-saving strategy? *Biological Journal of the Linnean Society*, 93:1–7. doi:10.1111/j.1095-8312.2007.00991.x.

Forni, K., ed.
2005. *The Chaucerian Apocrypha: A Selection.* Kalamazoo, MI: Medieval Institute Publications.

Foster, F. W.
1898. *A Bibliography of Skating.* London: B. W. Warhurst.

Fowler, G. H.
1897. *On the Outside Edge: Being Diversions in the History of Skating.* London: Horace Cox.

Fowler, G. H.
1909. Note on the early history of ski. *Year-Book of the Ski Club of Great Britain*, p. 62.

Fowler, G. H., ed.
1912. *Science of the Sea: An Elementary Handbook of Practical Oceanography for Travellers, Sailors, and Yachtsmen.* London: John Murray.

Fowler, G. H.
1922. *Bedfordshire in 1086: An Analysis and Synthesis of Domesday Book.* Aspley Guise: The Society.

Fowler, G. H.
1923. *The Care of County Muniments.* London: County Councils Association.

Fulton, J. H. W.
1911. *With Ski in Norway and Lapland.* London: P. L. Warner.

Garcin, J.
1813. *Le vrai patineur ou principes sur l'art de patiner avec grace.* Paris: J. Gillé.

Gassner, A.
1990. *Goethe als Eisläufer.* Frankfurt am Main: Peter Lang.

Goodman, N. and A. Goodman
1882. *Handbook of Fen Skating.* London: Sampson, Low, Marston, Searle, and Rivington.

Goubitz, O.
2000. Nederland's oudste schaats? *Kouwe Drukte,* 3(9):4–5.

Goubitz, O., C. van Driel-Murray, and W. G. van Waateringe
2001. *Stepping through Time: Archaeological Footwear from Prehistoric Times until 1800.* Zwolle, Netherlands: Stichting Promotie Archeologie.

Grimm, J. and W. Grimm
1998–2004. Das Deutsche Wörterbuch. Online.

Gutsmuths, J. C. F.
1793. *Gymnastik für die Jugend: Enthaltend eine praktische Anweisung zu Leibesübungen: Ein*

Beytrag zur nöthigsten Verbesserung der körperlichen Erziehung. Schnepfenthal: Buchhandlung der Erziehungsanstalt.

Gutsmuths, J. C. F.
1812. *Volledig leerstelsel van kunstmatige ligchaamsoefeningen, eene bijdrage tot de opvoeding der jeugde.* Leyden and Haarlem: Du Mortier en Loosjes.

Hagberg, U. E.
1976. Fundort und Fundgebiet der Modeln aus Torslunda. *Frühmittelalterliche Studien*, 10:323–349.

Halldór Halldórsson
1956. Leggir og skautar. In *Nordæla: Afæmliskveðja til Sigurðar Nordals*, Halldór Halldórsson, Steingrímur J. Þorsteinsson, Jón Jóhannesson, and Þorkell Jóhannesson, eds., pp. 75–89. Reykjavík: Helgafell.

Heathcote, J. M.
1892. The origin and development of skating. In *Skating*, Badminton Library of Sports and Pastimes, pp. 3–18. London: Longmans, Green, and Co.

Herman, O.
1902. Knochenschlittschuh, Knochenkufe, Knochenkeitel: Ein Beitrag zur näheren Kenntnis der prähistorischen Langknochenfunde. *Mittheilungen der anthropologischen Gesellschaft in Wien*, 32:217–238.

Hines, J. R.
2006. *Figure Skating: A History.* Urbana: University of Illinois Press.

Hines, J. R.
2008. *The English Style: Figure Skating's Oldest Tradition.* Westwood, MA: Neponset River Press.

Hines, J. R.
2011. *Historical Dictionary of Figure Skating.* Lanham, MD: Scarecrow Press.

Høegh-Guldberg, C.
1867. *Skøiteløberkunsten eller Anviisning til Skøiteløbning saavel for begyndere som Viderekomne.* Kopenhagen: Udgiverens Forlag i Ovist og Comp.s Bogtrykkeri.

Hoffman, L., ed.
1897. *Every Boy's Book of Sport and Pastime.* London: George Routledge and Sons, Ltd.

Hollander, L. M.
1964. *Snorri Sturluson. Heimskringla: History of the Kings of Norway.* Austin: University of Texas Press.

Holletschek, R.
1890. *Kunstfertigkeit im Eislaufen.* Troppau: Buchholz and Diebel.

Hoole, C.
1659. *J. A. Comenii. Orbis sensualium pictus.* London: n.p.

Huysmans, J.-K.
1923. *Saint Lydwine of Schiedam.* London: Kegan Paul, Trench, Trubner and Co., Ltd.

Ice Skating Institute
2012. *ISI Handbook*. Plano, TX: Ice Skating Institute.

Jón Jóhannesson, ed.
1950. *Austfirðinga sǫgur*, volume 11 of *Íslenzk fornrit*. Reykjavík: Hið íslenzka fornritafélag.

Jones, R.
1772. *A Treatise on Skating*. London: J. Ridley.

Jongen, L. and C. Schotel, eds.
1994. *Het leven van Liedewij, de maagd van Schiedam*, volume 2 of *Middelnederlandse Tekstedities*. Hilversum: Verloren.

Kayser, C. G., ed.
1834. *Index locupletissimus librorum qui inde ab anno MDCCL usque ad annum MDCCCXXXII in germania et in terris confinibus produierunt / Vollständiges Bücher-Lexicon enthaltend alle von 1750 bis zu Ende des Jahres 1831 in Deutschland und in den angrenzenden Ländern gedruckten Bücher*, volume 1. Leipzig: Ludwig Schumann.

Kluge, F. and E. Seebold, eds.
2002. *Etymologisches Wörterbuch der deutschen Sprache*, twenty-fourth edition. Berlin: Walter de Gruyter.

Kolodny, A.
2012. *In Search of First Contact: The Vikings of Vinland, the Peoples of the Dawnland, and the Anglo-American Anxiety of Discovery*. Durham, NC: Duke University Press.

Küchelmann, H. C.
2001–2011. Bone skates database. Online.

Küchelmann, H. C. and P. Zidarov
2005. Let's skate together! Skating on bones in the past and today. In *From Hooves to Horns, from Mollusc to Mammoth: Manufacture and Use of Bone Artefacts from Prehistoric Times to the Present, Proceedings of the 4th Meeting of the ICAZ Worked Bone Research Group at Tallinn, 26th–31st of August 2003*, H. Luik, A. M. Choyke, C. Batey, and L. Lõugas, eds., volume 15 of *Muinasaja Teadus*, pp. 425–445. Tallinn: Ajaloo Instituut.

Lambert, L.
1978. The American skating mania. *Journal of American Culture*, 1(4):683–698. doi:10.1111/j.1542-734X.1978.0104_683.x.

Lauwerier, R. C. G. M. and R. M. Van Heeringen
1998. Skates and prickers from the circular fortress of Oost-Souburg, the Netherlands (AD 900–975). *Environmental Archaeology*, 3:121–126. doi:10.1179/env.1998.3.1.121.

Lewis, J. F.
1895. *Skating and the Philadelphia Skating Club*. Philadelphia: n.p.

Liang, S.
1844. *Snorri Sturluson. Heimskringla or the Chronicle of the Kings of Norway*, release #15b, 1996 edition. Online Medieval and Classical Library.

MacGregor, A.
1975. Problems in the interpretation of microscopic wear patterns: The evidence from bone skates. *Journal of Archaeological Science*, 2:385–390.

MacGregor, A.
1985. *Bone, Antler, Ivory and Horn: The Technology of Skeletal Materials Since the Roman Period.* London: Croom Helm. Reprinted by Routledge in 2015.

Madan, F.
1877. Old German glosses from a Bodleian manuscript. *Journal of Philology*, 10:92–109.

Magnus, O.
1555. *Historia de gentibus septentrionalibus.* Rome: J. M. de Viottis.

Magnus, O.
1572. Carta marina et descriptio septentrionalium terrarum. Map.

Massie, R. K.
1980. *Peter the Great: His Life and His World.* New York: Alfred A. Knopf.

Member of the Skating Club
1831. *The Skater's Manual; or the Art of Skating, Now First Reduced to a Complete Practical System, with the Sets of Quadrilles as Skated on the Serpentine.* London: William Marsh.

Molema, H. and A. A. Ganderheyden
1985. *Woordenboek der Groningsche volkstaal in de 19de eeuw.* Groningen: Wolters-Noordhoff.

Monier-Williams, M. S. F. and S. F. Monier-Williams
1883. *Combined Figure Skating; Being a Collection of All the Known Combined Figures, Systematically Arranged, Named in Accordance with the Revised Code of "The Skating Club" London, and Illustrated by 130 Scaled Diagrams, Showing the Exact Method of Skating Each Figure; Together with a Progressive Series of Alternating "Calls."* London: Horace Cox.

Mulder, N.
2008a. Ten ijse (1). *Kouwe Drukte*, 12(33):25–30.

Mulder, N.
2008b. Ten ijse (2)—Schaatsles voor graaf Floris. *Kouwe Drukte*, 12(34):18–23.

Mulder, N.
2009a. Ten ijse (3)—Een steekpartij op scaverdinen? *Kouwe Drukte*, 13(35):27–31.

Mulder, N.
2009b. Ten ijse (4)—Met scaetzen en souerding op de hofgracht. *Kouwe Drukte*, 13(36):37–40.

Mulder, N.
2010. Ten ijse (6)—De revolutionaire puntschaats. *Kouwe Drukte*, 14(38):19–21.

Munro, R.
1894. Notes on ancient bone skates. *Proceedings of the Society of Antiquaries of Scotland*, 28:185–197.

Nichols, J., ed.
1801. *The Works of the Rev. Jonathan Swift*, volume 14. London: J. Johnson et al.

Paulin-Désormeaux, A. O.
1853. *Patinage et récréationes sur la glace*. Paris: Roret.

Piper, P., ed.
1882. *Die schriften Notkers und seiner Schule*. Freiburg i. B.: J. C. B. Mohr.

Randall, L. M. C.
1966. *Images in the Margins of Gothic Manuscripts*, volume 4 of *California Studies in the History of Art*. Berkeley: University of California Press.

Richardson, T. D.
1956. *Ice Skating*. London: B. T. Batsford, Ltd.

Robertson, J. C., ed.
1877. *Materials for the History of Thomas Becket, Archbishop of Canterbury*, volume 3. London: Longman.

Sahlstedt, A.
1773. *Svensk Ordbok*. Stockholm: Carl Stolpe.

Schlangenbogen, S.
1900. *Geschichte des Schlittschuhlaufens: Ein Beitrag zur Kenntniss der höheren Psychophysik.* n.p.: n.p.

Schützeichel, R., ed.
2004. *Althochdeutscher und Altsächsischer Glossenwortschatz.* Tübingen: Max Niemeyer Verlag.

Silva, A.
1857. *Sur le patin.* Paris: Librairie d'Alphonse Taride.

Smedley, E., H. J. Rose, and H. J. Rose, eds.
1845. *Encyclopædia Metropolitana: or Universal Dictionary of Knowledge*, volume 24. London: B. Fellowes et al.

Smith, C. R.
1848. Ancient bone skates. *Collectanea Antiqua*, 1:167–169.

Sordet, E.
1873. *Manuel du patineur: Nombreuses figures entièrement inédites.* Geneva: J.-G. Fick.

Stenberger, M.
1955. The finds and the dating of the Vallhagar settlement. In *Vallhagar: A Migration Period Settlement on Gotland, Sweden*, M. Stenberger and O. Klindt-Jensen, eds., volume 2, pp. 1065–1160. Copenhagen: Einar Munksgaards Forlag.

Stow, J.
1598. *A Survay of London: Contayning the Originall, Antiquity, Increase, Moderne Estate, and Description of that Citie: Written in the Yeare 1598.* London: John Wolfe.

Strauch, P., ed.
1919. *Paradisus anime intelligentis (Paradis der fornuftigen Sele).* Berlin: Weidmannsche Buchhandlung.

Stromberg, A. A., ed.
1914. *Esaias Tegnér. Fritiofs Saga.* Rock Island, IL: Augustana Book Concern. Republished by BiblioBazaar, Charleston, SC, 2006.

Swatek, W.
1877. *23 Tafeln enthaltend Schlittschuhlauf-Figuren und diverse Arten des Eislaufes.* Vienna: n.p.

Swift, F. and M. R. Clark
1868. *The Skater's Text Book.* New York: John A. Gray and Green.

ten Brink, H.
1880. *Der schnell perfecte und elegante Schlittschuhläufer, unentbehrliches Hülfsbüchlein für Freunde und Freundinnen des Eislaufs.* Harburg an der Elbe: Elkan.

Thurber, B. A.
2011. A new interpretation of Frithiof's steel shoes. *Scandinavica*, 50(2):6–30.

Thurber, B. A.
2013. The similarity of bone skates and skis. *Viking and Medieval Scandinavia*, 9:199–217. doi:10.1484/J.VMS.1.103882.

Thurber, B. A., ed.
2017. *R. Jones. A Treatise on Skating.* Evanston, IL: Skating History Press.

Trichter, V.
1742. *Curiöses Reit-Jagd-Fecht-Tanz-oder Ritter-Exercitien Lexicon.* Leipzig: J. F. Gleditsch.

Trunz, E., ed.
1948. *Goethes Werke: Hamburger Ausgabe in 14 Bänden*, volume 9. Hamburg: C. Wegner.

Urban, S.
1853. A midland town in the reign of George the Third. *The Gentleman's Magazine*, pp. 28–33.

Urdahl, L.
1891. *Norsk idræt: Skildringer og skisser fra norsk sportsliv.* Christiania: A. Cammermeyer.

van Buttingha Wichers, J.
1888. *Schaatsenrijden.* 's-Gravenhage: W. Cremer.

Vandervell, H. E. and T. M. Witham
1869. *A System of Figure-Skating: Being the Theory and Practice of the Art as Developed in England, with a Glance at Its Origin and History*, first edition. London: Macmillan and Co.

Vandervell, H. E. and T. M. Witham
1874. *A System of Figure-Skating: Being the Theory and Practice of the Art as Developed in England, with a Glance at Its Origin and History*, second edition. London: Horace Cox.

Vandervell, H. E. and T. M. Witham
1880. *A System of Figure-Skating: Being the Theory and Practice of the Art as Developed in England, with a Glance at Its Origin and History*, third edition. London: Horace Cox.

Verwijs, E., J. Verdam, W. de Vreese, G. I. Lieftinck, and A. A. Beekman
1990. *Middelnederlandsch woordenboek*. Zedelgem: Flandra Nostra.

Vieth, G. U. A.
1789. Ueber das Schrittschuhlaufen: Ein Versuch, in einer Gesellschaft von Freunden vorgelesen. *Neue Litteratur und Völkerkunde*, 3(1):100–126.

Vieth, G. U. A.
1794. *Versuch einer Encyklopädie der Leibesübungen*. Berlin: C. L. Hartman.

Virchow, R.
1870. Geglättete Knochen zum Gebrauche beim Schlittschuhlaufen und Weben. *Verhandlungen der Berliner Gesellschaft für Anthropologie, Ethnologie und Vorgeschichte*, pp. 19–21. In *Zeitschrift für Ethnologie* 3 (1871).

Virchow, R.
1887. Einige Ueberlebsel in pommerschen Gebräuchen. *Verhandlungen der Berliner Gesellschaft für Anthropologie, Ethnologie und Vorgeschichte*, pp. 361–362. In *Zeitschrift für Ethnologie* 19 (1887).

Wawn, A.
2000. *The Vikings and the Victorians: Inventing the Old North in Nineteenth-Century Britain*. Woodbridge: Boydell and Brewer.

William H. Schab Gallery
1967. *Early Texts and Illustrated Books: Arts and Sciences of Six Centuries*. New York: W. H. Schab.

Winroth, A.
2014. *The Age of the Vikings*. Princeton, NJ: Princeton University Press.

Wirth, M.
1868. Der Eislauf. *Die Gartenlaube*, 16:806–808, 823–824.

Witham, T. M.
1895. Skating gossip. *The Badminton Magazine*, 1:608–613.

Ytter, F.
1868. *Kroppsöfningar och lekar*. Örebrö: Abr. Bohlin.

Zähler, J.
1866. *Das Schlittschuhlaufen. Für Jung und Alt bei-*

derlei Geschlechts methodisch dargestellt von Julius Zähler, Oberlehrer am Vitzthum'schen Gymnasium in Desden. Leipzig: J. J. Weber.

Zindel, C. S.
1825. *Der Eislauf.* Nürnberg: Friedrich Campe.

Illustration credits

Cover Magnus (1572), courtesy of WikiMedia Commons.

I Fowler (1897:frontispiece), courtesy of Harvard University Library.

C1 Anonymous (1861:159), photographed by B. A. Thurber at the Newberry Library in Chicago, IL.

C2 Smith (1848:167), scanned by B. A. Thurber from the microfilm at Northwestern University in Evanston, IL.

C3 Heathcote (1892:5), digitized by Google Books.

C4 Munro (1894:186), digitized by Google Books.

C5 Virchow (1887:362), digitized by Google Books.

C6 Magnus (1555:713), digitized by Google Books.

C7 Magnus (1555:122), digitized by Google Books.

C8 Brugman (1498:n.p.), courtesy of WikiMedia Commons.

C9 Herman (1902:220), digitized by Google Books.

C10 Balduinus and Nigronus (1667:facing p. 40), digitized by Google Books.

C11 William H. Schab Gallery (1967:43), courtesy of WikiMedia Commons.

Index